Fantasies of Hong Kong Disneyland

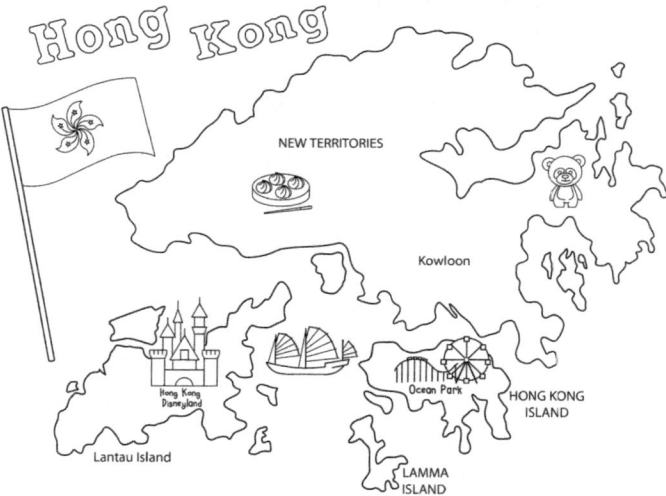

FRONTISPIECE. Map of Hong Kong.

Fantasies of Hong Kong Disneyland

Attempted Indigenizations of Space, Labor, and Consumption

JENNY BANH

Rutgers University Press
New Brunswick, Camden, and Newark, New Jersey
London and Oxford

Rutgers University Press is a department of Rutgers, The State University of New Jersey, one of the leading public research universities in the nation. By publishing worldwide, it furthers the University's mission of dedication to excellence in teaching, scholarship, research, and clinical care.

Library of Congress Cataloging-in-Publication Data
Names: Banh, Jenny, author.
Title: Fantasies of Hong Kong Disneyland : attempted indigenizations of space, labor, and consumption / Jenny Banh.
Description: New Brunswick, New Jersey : Rutgers University Press, 2025. | Includes bibliographical references and index.
Identifiers: LCCN 2024039625 | ISBN 9780813593449 (paperback) | ISBN 9780813593456 (cloth) | ISBN 9780813593463 (epub) | ISBN 9780813593487 (pdf)
Subjects: LCSH: Hong Kong Disneyland (Hong Kong, China) | International business enterprises—Social aspects—China—Hong Kong. | Social change—China—Hong Kong. | Culture diffusion—China—Hong Kong. | Popular culture—China—Hong Kong—American influences. | Popular culture and globalization—China—Hong Kong.
Classification: LCC GV1853.4.C62 H633 2025 | DDC 338.4/779106885125—dc23/eng/20241107
LC record available at https://lccn.loc.gov/2024039625

A British Cataloging-in-Publication record for this book is available from the British Library.

Copyright © 2025 by Jenny Banh
All rights reserved
No part of this book may be reproduced or utilized in any form or by any means, electronic or mechanical, or by any information storage and retrieval system, without written permission from the publisher. Please contact Rutgers University Press, 106 Somerset Street, New Brunswick, NJ 08901. The only exception to this prohibition is "fair use" as defined by U.S. copyright law.

References to internet websites (URLs) were accurate at the time of writing. Neither the author nor Rutgers University Press is responsible for URLs that may have expired or changed since the manuscript was prepared.

∞ The paper used in this publication meets the requirements of the American National Standard for Information Sciences—Permanence of Paper for Printed Library Materials, ANSI Z39.48-1992.
rutgersuniversitypress.org

Contents

	List of Illustrations	vii
	Preface	ix
	Abbreviations	xv
	Introduction	1
1.	Indigenizing Consumption: Culture Wars	25
2.	Labor Indigenization: Cultural Imperialist Attitudes	55
3.	Spatial Indigenization: Creating a Heterotopia	73
4.	An Indigenous Competitor: Ocean Park	99
	Epilogue	115
	Postscript: Fairytale Endings	120
	Acknowledgments	125
	Notes	129
	References	131
	Index	155

Illustrations

Maps

Frontispiece.	Map of Hong Kong	ii
1.	Hong Kong Disneyland	75
2.	Ocean Park	102

Figures

1.	Hong Kong history timeline	7
2–5.	Hong Kong Disneyland timeline	16–19
6.	Hong Kong Disneyland attendance 2006–2022	22
7.	Hong Kong Disneyland attendance 2008–2022: Local Hong Konger, mainland Chinese, and international	28
8.	Hong Kong Disneyland annual profit/loss 2006–2022	67
9.	Cable car view	100
10.	Hong Kong Disneyland and Ocean Park attendance 2006–2023	109

Drawings

1. People are magic — x
2. Hong Kong schoolgirls holding their ground — 27
3. HKDL gate — 56
4. HKDL coin — 83
5. Asian people in Victorian Park — 88
6. HKDL wishing well — 90
7. HKDL Mystic Manor — 91
8. Victorian nightmare — 92
9. Dead fish — 97
10. McDull in Old Time Hong Kong Area in Ocean Park — 106
11. Forever playing in the Enchanted Forest — 118
12. Spreading Asian Joy and Love — 122

Tables

1. List of interviewees — 58
2. HKDL labor grievances — 70
3. Five elements of feng shui at HKDL — 80
4. Feng shui colors at HKDL — 82
5. Feng shui numerology — 84
6. Ocean Park's and Hong Kong Disneyland's values, compared — 108

Preface

Let me tell you a little story about myself.

I am an ethnic Chinese from Vietnam who migrated to Ferguson, Missouri, and later Belleville, Illinois, where I went to all-Anglo Catholic School and worked in a Chinese restaurant where all my customers were working-class African Americans and Anglos. It was the 1980s, and there was massive racial animosity between groups because of social and economic inequalities.

Read between the lines here. POC [people of color] or minorities you know....

I had to appease the priests and nuns during the day, African American customers after school, and then my war refugee parents with PTSD (posttraumatic stress disorder) at night. On the ground, I learned that these three groups had different and overlapping wants and that to "serve" them I had to be nimble. This is probably why I have wanted to be an anthropologist since I was eight years old. I also watched daily PBS, *Star Trek*, and weekend WWE (World Wrestling Entertainment), which had an effect.

DRAWING 1. People are magic. (Credit: Sally Pirie.)

I learned that people are magic.

In anthropology, when the local population takes outside products and makes it their own, we call the process *indigenization*. I did the reverse, as I was a stranger, and I adjusted to these disparate groups. But in reality, I just wanted to avoid or ignore the daily microaggressions, spankings from irate nuns, and being screamed at by my survival-mode parents.

I was subconsciously code-switching my life away to survive. Despite my best efforts, I got spanked a lot and yelled at, which made me try to adjust myself further "to serve" or internally (reverse) *indigenize* to these groups. This is why I am always uncomfortable.

> *Even while writing that sentence, I am uncomfortable, thinking this reader is going to judge me and after this sentence will decide whether to read on or drop this book.*

My family is not "authentically" Chinese because we spent three generations in Vietnam. As a result, we guessed about how to cook American Chinese food for our midwestern customers. While fleeing from the war, we stopped by Hong Kong for a short while before coming to the United States. Yes, the family secret is that we fled to Hong Kong and left Vietnam. My parents lied to me my whole life and told me I was *just* from Hong Kong, never mentioning our family's seventy years in Vietnam (Banh 2019a). I spent three months in Hong Kong as an infant before I came back as an adult graduate student researcher. But I was an obedient, plaid-skirt-wearing girl like the cartoon Meilin "Mei" Lee in *Turning Red* (2022), so I believed my parents.

> *Yes, I identify with a cartoon: she is ME in so many ways.*

She wears a hair clip, leggings, plaid skirt, and Mary Janes and has her Tamagotchi by her side. Her constant strained smiling masks her discomfort (and agony). She evades her parents, has a Canadianized all-girl friendship group, and loves boy bands. But I never let my inner panda get out like she did. The bane of my existence is that I have internalized the Catholic school system panopticon and that I am always yearning for those worthless white award ribbons that the nuns gave out.

Is this book my ribbon now?

Our Chinese restaurant was a converted gas station, and we lived in the back. We made food like the St. Paul sandwich, which was a gigantic egg patty between two slices of white bread. Crab rangoon was a cheese and fake crab monstrosity that customers enjoyed. Even when I was nine, I always laughed (inside) when I took orders for the Pu Pu Platter. Nothing we served would be recognizable to mainland Chinese palates. We used local ingredients and adapted to the local environment. We never ate anything we served our customers unless they forgot to pick up their orders. In the 1990s, my father decided that we would have a better life in California, and we packed up our very few belongings and landed in upper-middle-class Diamond Bar, California, where wealthy Latinos, Anglos, African Americans, and Asian Americans had settled.

We left our dog Xiao-Bi, which makes me sad to think about.

These rich people saw life differently and had different consumption, labor, and space patterns. Again, they were nothing like my working-class family, who worked with their hands and were uncouth in many ways. Whether my relatives were speaking Cantonese, Mandarin, or Vietnamese, their speech always sounded uneducated, but they were good at making money.[1] My new Diamond Bar friends were wealthy transnational Asian Americans who took constant trips back and forth to Korea, Hong Kong, and Japan. I learned how to be "Asian" from my thirteen-year-old Korean best friend Jennifer, who had recently arrived in the United States.

Like most Orange County and San Gabriel Valley middle schoolers, we went to Disneyland yearly. I liked it, but not as much as I loved Transformers and Strawberry Shortcake. Then in 1992 the LA riots hit, and in my sixth-period class, the Korean American students were screaming and crying. They blamed the violence on African Americans. I disagreed, but I did not have the language to explain structural or historical racism and its effects. The television showed LA buildings burning and Korean Americans defending their stores. It was a racial infotainment of Asian Americans pitted against African American. The Model Minority Myth in full swing.

What they did not show was this was another example of African Americans again being denied justice. Ethnic middlemen bear the brunt of global racial capitalist inequality, and that is why my family fled Vietnam. The rich Beverly Hills people were fully defended. The origins of the racial tensions were multivariate and would fill another book.

So much intergenerational pain.

When I got home my parents were screaming at me as they could not find me. I was editing the school newspaper, and there was not the 24/7 communication that we have now. The LA riots triggered primordial fears in them, and they were ready to run. My whole family have our passports nearby.

Just a kid.

I saw firsthand what happens when local communities are not listened to and destruction can ensue. One could say my interest in the "community" started here.

Perhaps? I don't know.

Like many first- or 1.5-generation Americans, I was always told to protect the family first, and that is what I did. This led me to have an interest in African American studies, Asian American studies (at-large ethnic studies), and Asian studies. I also love pop culture, like *Monchhichis*, Rainbow Bright, hip-hop, and all things Marvel. McDull, Space Ghost, and Dune make me dream of a better world. So when Disney came to Hong Kong, I wanted to see Disney's indigenization practices, and I also wanted to go back to a place I left when I was three months old. I wanted to see if Disney really did indigenize or listen to the local Hong Kong community, which is what they claimed.

This is a small work to show

Hong Kong Matters

A Beginning

Disney fans: Why don't you write me a book for me to read?

Abbreviations

CDL	California Disneyland
HK	Hong Kong
HKDL	Hong Kong Disneyland
MTR	Mass Transit Railway
OP	Ocean Park
SAR	Special Administrative Region
TDL	Tokyo Disneyland

Fantasies of Hong Kong Disneyland

Introduction

I walk under the green Hong Kong Disneyland sign that reads "Welcome to Hong Kong Disneyland Resort" (in Chinese). The immaculate ground is made of asphalt. I see a metal Mickey Mouse surfing on the water spouting from a metal whale. We are enclosed on the sides by walls of green foliage, blocking our view like the walls of a prison. The buildings, simulacra of an early twentieth-century New England town globally known as Disney Main Street USA, look eerily new. The stores, like the parking lot, are almost empty. The food vendors do not have crowds clamoring to buy their curry fish balls wrapped in plastic. Where are all the tourists? I hear a local Hong Konger tell a friend that the rival Hong Kong theme park called Ocean Park is much better. Extensive Disney public relations materials tell me that HKDL is "culturally sensitive" (or indigenized) to Hong Kong local culture. They neglect to tell us that the park was built on undetonated World War II bombs.[1]

English, Mandarin, and Cantonese voices clamor to be heard. Off to the side, a small mainland Chinese boy urinates into a bush shaped like Mickey Mouse. Haggard Hong Kong Disneyland "cast members" rush to the child, trying to persuade the parents (using faux Beijing accents promoting ersatz Chinese solidarity) to stop the child's behavior. The mainland Chinese parents do not understand and button up the square flap of the toddler's overalls to cover his bare bottom. A local Hong Kong woman, offended by this scene, screams at the boy in ear-piercing Cantonese (field notes 2010).

I hear giggles and see a huge crowd gather. A group of young Asian women or teens with Fox Ears headbands are taking multiple selfies while holding a gigantic pink stuffed fox called LinaBell. (She is part of the Duffy and Friends collection.) The women are wearing dresses with white and light blue Victorian puffed sleeves with ruffle elastic cuffs. Some of them wear all-white dresses that look like miniskirt wedding gowns. Some are wearing kawaii Alice in Wonderland–inspired princess dresses with huge, puffed sleeves and petticoats. Others wear snap-on LinaBell tails. They are waiting eagerly in line for the larger-than-human-sized character CookieAnn. CookieAnn, a dog chef, is the only uniquely Hong Kong character in Duffy and Friends. CookieAnn puts both paws on her face and tilts her body to the right. She stretches out her arms and bends her paw feet. Her handlers wait on both sides of her so the squealing attendees do not rush toward her after she is done. This cuteness overwhelms us, and after her presentation, I buy a CookieAnn headband and promise myself that next time I will show up in a black Victorian kawaii Alice in Wonderland dress (field notes 2023).

The first vignette is a scene I observed time and time again at Hong Kong Disneyland (HKDL; Chinese: 香港迪士尼樂園), featuring intercultural Chinese conflict, attempted space localization, and questionable consumption adaptations at the park. The second vignette illustrates how HKDL adjusts its products to meet the needs of local and international guests, in this case by incorporating Duffy and Friends products from Tokyo Disneyland. Although Hong Kong

Disneyland is similar in many ways to the original California Disneyland theme park, the efforts to adapt it to its local context tell a fascinating story of attempted indigenization.

This book examines the attempt to transplant Disney's "happiest place on earth" to Hong Kong, with complicated results. Focusing on the theme of attempted indigenization (localization) in a globalized transnational park, it shows how complex transnational labor relations, competing local theme park attractions, and intracultural conflicts have complicated the process of indigenization. At HKDL, citizens of the powerful People's Republic of China (PRC) and the corporate behemoth Disney come together in the third space of Hong Kong. The situation poses special challenges for Disney's efforts to manage space, labor, and consumption to achieve local adaptation and business success.

This book argues that Hong Kong Disneyland has attempted to indigenize the local Hong Kong culture in the areas of space, labor, and consumption but has done so unevenly and with limited success. HKDL indigenization (or accommodation to the local culture) foundered, I show, because of the unequal original contract between Disney and the government of the Hong Kong Special Autonomous Region (SAR) and because of worker and community distrust for the organization. HKDL also failed notably to account for local interethnic conflicts. As James Scott argues in *Seeing Like a State* (1998), state projects that are high modernist must take into account local population conditions and differences. Disney is an example of a high modernist transnational corporation that has clear labor, space, and consumption rules. This book traces the web that connects and constrains the small world of Hong Kong Disneyland: Hong Kong's cultural and political transformations, the relative rigidity of Disney's global corporate cultural machine, and the Chinese mainland state's developmental strategies. Hong Kong Disneyland is not merely a space of play; rather, it is a space that reveals much about international tensions between East and West and intranational tensions among different Chinese publics.

Hong Kong Disneyland: The Experience

Hong Kong Disneyland opened on September 12, 2005. It was built on Lantau Island, Penny's Bay. The park is small compared to other Disney parks, spanning 68 acres within the larger 310-acre resort. To enter the park, visitors walk underneath a green sign that reads "Welcome to Hong Kong Disneyland Resort." Following a lengthy wait to pass through security, they encounter a gigantic Mickey Mouse face made of bright flowers. After navigating dozens of selfie-takers in front of the flowered Mickey, they have the option to enter one of two dark tunnels. Once through a tunnel, the visitors see Main Street USA, a familiar site to most Disney fans because it is a carbon copy of the original Main Street USA built at California Disneyland (CDL).

Main Street USA is paved with red tiles. Like visitors to Main Street USA at other parks, visitors here are funneled into the Emporium store, which here is filled with a cornucopia of Duffy and Friends T-shirts, stuffed animals of various sizes, and Lotso Bears strawberry dresses. Mulan is nowhere to be found. Unlike many Disney stores, Mickey Mouse–branded items compete with Duffy and Friends–branded items; the latter are particularly popular in Japan and China. Throughout the park, guests wear customized Duffy and Friends animal ear headbands featuring the entire Duffy crew.

Echoing the layout of other Disney parks, the exit from Main Street USA offers a choice among six thematic "lands," including the familiar Disney mainstays Tomorrowland, Fantasyland, and Adventureland as well as some new additions: Grizzly Gulch, Mystic Point, and Toy Story Land. Again like in other parks, Main Street USA sits opposite a fairytale castle. However, in recent years Hong Kong Disneyland has replaced the original castle with a new "Castle of Magical Dreams" that is noticeably bigger than its California Disneyland counterpart. The HKDL variation is also characterized by its pastel blend of pink, gold, blue, and green. The castle is a popular magnet for photo seekers. On one typical visit to HKDL with my family, we decided to skip the photo-op and turn right, passing the Main Street USA throne and various Cantonese food stalls selling Mickey-themed food and heading to Tomorrowland. Once there, we saw a layout that is replicated in the other lands: a couple of rides, land-specific themed restaurants and stores, performance areas, and, on this day, long lines.

From Tomorrowland we made our way counter-clockwise through the park, moving through Fantasyland, Toy Story Land, the Victorian/colonial-themed Mystic Point, and the American West–themed Grizzly Gulch, before ending up in Adventureland. Each land features the familiar Disney attention to detail in everything from rides to bathroom fixtures. HKDL has expanded over the past decade, but it is still noticeably smaller than CDL. On less crowded days, one can easily cover the park while hitting most of the major rides in half a day. During our visit, the park was so crowded that nearly all rides had wait times of more than an hour, often in fully or partially exposed heat and with only the occasional fan to provide minimal relief. But neither the sauna-level heat nor the crowds seemed to dampen the enthusiasm of the park guests.

Finally, we left the rides to hunt for a meal. HKDL offers fairly diverse food options, balanced between standard American park fare and local favorites. Among other options, park guests can choose between expensive hot dogs, hamburgers, Vietnamese pho, Singaporean laksa soup, Indian-style butter chicken, and various plant-based options. I chose the satisfying laksa soup, and we hit a few final rides before making our way to the park's signature multimedia fireworks show, "Momentous Nighttime Spectacular," which bills itself as storytelling with magic, light, and sound. During the show, the Castle of Magical Dreams is transformed into a canvas for nostalgic videos made up of popular Disney films and characters, all supported by familiar Disney earworms, with a loud and colorful fireworks display to end the night. As the show ended, the throngs of park guests were funneled toward the single exit. Once outside the park, we ran as fast as we could alongside other local Hong Konger park guests and HKDL workers to the MTR (Mass Transit Railroad) gate to try to catch the train back to Hong Kong before it closed. The train eventually deposited us at the Sunny Bay MTR station, where we ran up the stairs and across the connecting overpass at a breakneck speed to avoid the human deluge trying to catch the connecting train. We made it. And then we laughed and remembered the dozens of times we had made the same run.

A Troubled History

A primer on Hong Kong's recent history is a useful entry point for understanding HKDL's history. In short, Hong Kong's economic woes opened the door to the Hong Kong government's nontransparent dealings with Disney as they negotiated the terms for the opening of HKDL. The Hong Kong government's confidence took a dip after 1997, when a number of expats and Hong Kong residents emigrated to other parts of the world (Sussman 2010). In an attempt to revive the economy, Tung Chee Hwa, then Hong Kong's top official chief executive and president of the Executive Council after the handover, endorsed a deal to bring the Disney theme park to the city.

The story, however, begins further back in history. In 1839, Britain and mainland China went to war over opium and

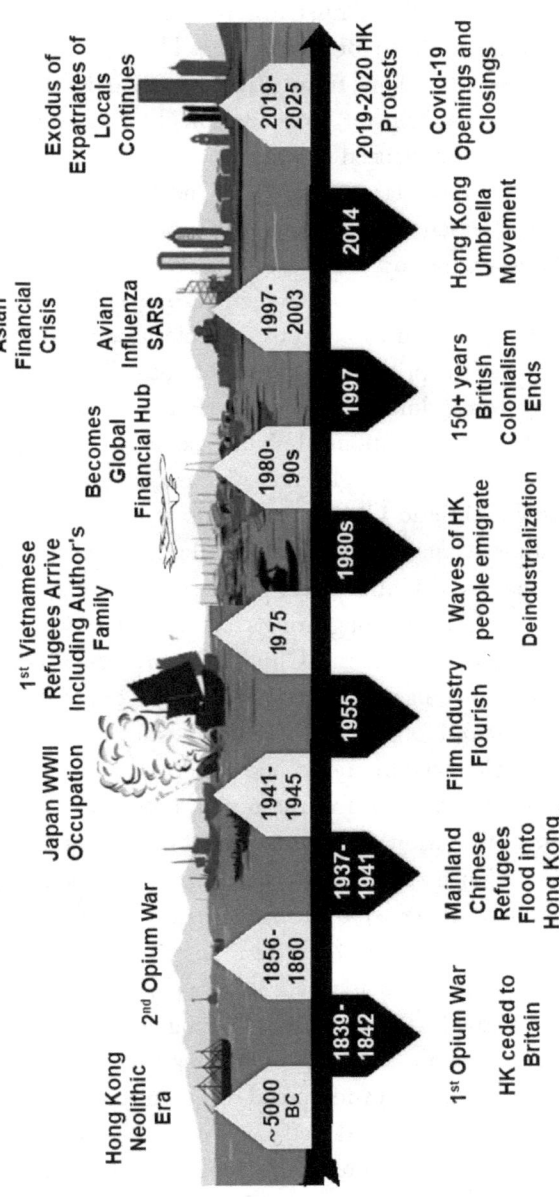

FIGURE 1. Hong Kong history timeline. (Credit: Viviana Moyano.)

trading rights. After China lost the First Opium War, it ceded Hong Kong to Britain in 1842. Hong Kong was formally a British colony from 1842 to 1997 and served as a bastion of capitalism for Great Britain. During this period, Hong Kong experienced significant economic development, billing itself as a place where "East meets West"—an ideal location in which to do business. As Hong Kong industrialized between the 1950s and the 1980s, its residents provided the labor necessary to produce such desirable global goods as plastic flowers, transistor radios, and clothing. The garment industry was the primary employer for both men and women in Hong Kong during this period (Pang, Lang, and Chiu 2001). As an international hub for exchange, Hong Kong came to be known as a "global city" (Sassen 2001).

After mainland China opened up in the 1980s, Hong Kong underwent a rapid deindustrialization: because factories in mainland China could produce the same goods at a fraction of the cost, Hong Kong's factories were closed down and relocated to mainland China. The process of deindustrialization was marked by the notable drop in the manufacturing share of Hong Kong's gross domestic product (GDP). It is also evidenced by the 30 percent decline in the number of manufacturing jobs, from 50,606 in 1988 to 33,863 in 1994 and the elimination of close to 500,000 jobs between 1987 and 1995 (Census and Statistics Department 1988, 1996). As the manufacturing sector declined, the service sector burgeoned. The tourism and service industries rapidly took the place of the garment industry in Hong Kong, although at the cost of the loss of many jobs (Leung 2001).

When Britain's "lease" of Hong Kong expired in July 1997, China took over amid widespread social upheaval since many Hong Kongers who had fled communist mainland China dreaded the prospect of returning to China's political system. Others—especially businesspeople—had already left Hong

Kong in the 1980s, frightened by the expected return of Hong Kong to China, although many returned later with foreign passports (Sussman 2010). This exodus and the accompanying capital flight were a negative development for Hong Kong laborers: thousands of men and women were fired from their jobs when businesspeople moved their factories to mainland China. The combination of rising unemployment rates and decreasing wages produced significant hardship among Hong Kong's working classes.

When Hong Kong was taken back by China, it became part of the "One Country, Two Systems" arrangement, according to which Hong Kong would retain its capitalist system under the umbrella of China's communist rule for fifty years after the handover (Chan and Postiglione 1996). Hong Kong's labor problems, however, were far from over, and they were exacerbated by the 2002–2004 severe acute respiratory syndrome (SARS) pandemic, the H_5N_1 avian flu outbreaks of 1997, and the 1997 Asian financial crisis. The avian influenza outbreak negatively impacted Hong Kong labor and tourism: "The human case attracted considerable international attention" (Sims and Peiris 2013). By the time of the handover from Great Britain to China, Hong Kong was far from an ideal place financially, politically, and economically. It was around this time that the Walt Disney Company brokered a deal with HK's state government.

Precedents: Other Disneylands

To understand how the troubled Hong Kong came to host a Disneyland and why the deal unfolded the way it did, it is essential to consider not only Hong Kong's political and economic environment in the 1990s but also the lessons Disney had learned from the creation of other Disneylands. After visiting Griffith Park with his daughters, Walt Disney was inspired to build a safe, wondrous place for adults and children. This friendly place would not serve alcohol or allow any of the seedy elements of carnivals. The original park was located next to Burbank, California, and was called Mickey Mouse Park; it eventually moved to Anaheim, California. Anaheim Disneyland opened on July 17, 1955. An expansion, California Adventure Park, opened on February 8, 2001.

The success of the first Disneyland led to the opening of a second park in Florida. The Walt Disneyworld Resort opened on October 1, 1971, on over 305 acres of land in Bay Lake, Florida. Eventually it grew to include the Magic Kingdom (October 1, 1971), EPCOT (October 1, 1982), Disney Hollywood Studio (May 1, 1989), and Disney's Animal Kingdom (April 22, 1998).

According to ReviewTyme, by the 1980s the Disney theme parks were generating 70 percent of the Walt Disney Company's revenue. As a result, Disney executives began to think about possibilities for international expansion. On April 15, 1983, the company partnered with Oriental Land Company (OLC) to create Tokyo Disneyland (東京ディズニーランド) in Urayasu, Japan, a vast theme park that paid royalty fees to the Walt Disney Company. It was a tremendous success, drawing very high local Japanese and Asian regional attendance. Aviad Raz (1999) argues that the park is culturally suited to Japanese tastes but portrays itself as quintessentially American, which is one of the secrets to its success. It uses the standard Japanese labor system and does not have vending machines, so in many ways Tokyo Disneyland (TDL) is a quintessential Japanese company. The Japanese love of kawaii ("cute culture") means that Disney items fit well into Japanese cultural consumption patterns. In a sense, however, TDL was a missed financial opportunity for the Walt Disney Company: because the park is fully owned by the Oriental Land Company, Disney does not receive the full profits (Raz 1999). Nevertheless, the success of TDL led to the opening in 2001 of the most profitable Disney Park in the world, Tokyo DisneySea, a marine park.

The next international park to appear was Euro Disneyland, which opened in Chessey, France, on April 12, 1992, to unprecedented controversy, with a flood of bad publicity and charges of American cultural imperialism. French movie director Ariane Mnouchkine famously called the site a "cultural Chernobyl" because it encouraged excessive U.S. commercialism and consumption and served alcohol-free mocktails.

Tony Baxter, former senior vice president of creative development for Walt Disney Imagineering, argues that they took American themes like Main Street USA to be more French and European (Baxter 1992, 62–71). "Research showed that the Europeans, and particularly the French felt that the American approach was too shallow, and that we [Imagineering] needed to temper down the commercial aspect of the presentation. . . . On Main Street, we wanted to create the atmosphere of an American town, but we cannot expect everyone to understand that imagery so we tried to tell more of a story, to create a little more romance" (Baxter 1992, 65, quoted in Mittermeier 2021, 112). Predictably, the park failed to reach its projected attendance and profit levels.

Roger Cohen of the *New York Times* quoted a statement by the French park: "'Throughout fiscal year 1994, Euro Disney will require significant funding. Should the financial restructuring not be completed, the company would face a liquidity problem.' A lack of liquidity implies insufficient cash or credit to pay bills or other obligations. In the extreme form, it can lead to bankruptcy," he concluded (Cohen 1993). A Saudi Arabian prince intervened by infusing cash into the park to keep it financially viable (Mittermeier 2021, 146). Because the French associated the term "Euro" with cold commerce, the park was renamed Disneyland Paris in an effort to rehabilitate its image. The park still has well-publicized public relations and profitability issues as well as seasonality issues.

The disastrous Euro Disneyland opening was overseen by Disney CEO Michael Eisner, who had been hired to replace Ron Miller, Walt Disney's son-in-law, in September 1984, soon after the opening of Tokyo Disneyland. During his tenure, Eisner built up the company by spearheading blockbuster animations such as *The Little Mermaid* (1989), *Aladdin* (1992), and *The Lion King* (1994). He developed Disney MGM Studies (1989) and Disney Animal Kingdom (1998) in Orlando, Florida. Eisner oversaw the success of TDL and was involved in the opening of Disneyland Paris (1992), Tokyo DisneySea (2001), and Hong Kong Disneyland (2005). Eisner watched the TDL success—which, as mentioned before, was something of a missed opportunity for Disney—and the Disneyland Paris failure closely. When Disney entered Hong Kong, Eisner was determined not to repeat the company's cultural, labor, and economic mistakes.

Talks about HKDL Begin

Talks about Disneyland coming to Hong Kong began in 1997 after the British government ceded control of Hong Kong Island back to mainland China. The talks included an initial discussion of the possibility of bringing Disneyland to mainland China, but this idea fell through after Disney backed Martin Scorsese's film *Kundun* (1997), which dramatized the life of the Dalai Lama and China's invasion of Tibet. "Disney had previously hoped to build in Shanghai, but talks there broke off not long after the 1996 release of Martin Scorsese's 'Kundun' which was critical of China's policy in Tibet" (Frater 2005). Hong Kong, however, was another story. Because China and Hong Kong followed two different economic-political frameworks, as described earlier—communism on the mainland and capitalism in the Hong Kong territories—Hong Kong was not directly under the mainland's economic jurisdiction. Culturally, Hong Kong was much more Western than China and more accepting of political disagreements. Although the doors were closed to the mainland, Hong Kong remained a viable site for a new Disney theme park.

The location of any new Disney theme park typically involves competition. In the case of Euro Disney, the company expertly pitted Paris against London and Madrid. Eventually, with many public concessions that Parisians continued to complain about afterward, the park went to France. In the intense negotiations that surround the choice of a location, Disney is frequently able to obtain free or greatly discounted government property or private land and transportation and infrastructure assistance. For Hong Kong Disneyland, as was the case for Shanghai Disneyland, Disneyworld in Florida, and Disneyland Paris, the government offered economic concessions in exchange for building a park. In a deal that will be described in the next section, Hong Kong was selected as the site for the next Disneyland.

Disney's Unequal Deal with the Hong Kong Government

When HKDL was under discussion, critics expressed two central reservations about the proposed park, one environmental and the other about labor. One fear was that Disney would create low-quality jobs. Disney responded that many high-quality technical jobs would be created. Another concern was that the location of the park would disturb the fragile Penny Bay ecosystem (Choy 2011). These concerns will be discussed in greater depth in the chapters on space and labor. Despite such objections, the deal went forward.

According to the agreement between the Walt Disney Company and the Hong Kong government that was reached on October 31, 1999, Hong Kong Disneyland would be owned and operated by Hong Kong International Theme Park Limited, which would be jointly owned by Disney and the Hong Kong government (Hong Kong Government 1999). However, the deal was inequitable from the start. In a major point of controversy between the company and the government, the Hong Kong SAR paid 90 percent of the infrastructure construction costs for the new park but secured only a slight majority (57 percent) of shares in the project, with no executive privileges and no copyrights on merchandise (Hong Kong Disneyland 2011).

The contract stipulated that the Hong Kong government would invest US$2.9 billion (HK$23 billion) for a 57 percent equity stake and Disney would invest US$316 million (HK$2.45 billion) for a 43 percent equity stake (Hills and Welford 2006). Disney therefore contributed only around 10 percent of the total cost, even though the project was supposed to require an equal monetary commitment from both parties. As one of my interviewees joked, "Disney laughingly told its Anaheim, California, shareholders they got a free theme park!" (interview with HKDL worker 2010). According to an article in the *South China Morning Post*, "The deal between the Hong Kong government and Walt Disney has long been labelled an 'unequal treaty,' which sees the American parent company receive millions in potential profits while the city's taxpayers are left to foot most of the park's bills" (Sun 2017). Sun (2017) also reported that HKDL had to pay royalties and management fees even if it lost money. Frater (2005) writes, "$417 million of equity, the government has provided loans of $1 billion and invested $1.7 billion in capital projects such as land reclamation and building the new spur for the subway. Disney, on the other hand, put up

$371 million for its 43 percent equity stake and will earn management fees for running the show."

Over the next six years, the park was built with Hong Kong government investments totaling HK$22.45 billion (US$2.88 billion). (For a timeline of the park, see figures 2–5.) The total cost of construction was US$3.5 billion. The agreement between the HK government and Disney also specified that "the government would hold subordinated shares that would convert to ordinary shares, raising the government's ownership as high as 75% if the park did much better than originally envisioned" (Bradsher 2004).

Figures 2 to 5 provide a historical snapshot of the events that led to the creation of the theme park. They begin with the governmental negotiations and political climate. There are notable dates such as the groundbreaking and evolution of the park. The figures also include rides and castles that were developed and then redeveloped.

According to Lyne (2004), in 2004 the projected total cost of HKDL was US$3.5 billion (US$1.81 billion construction costs, US$1.74 billion site buying and development). Initially it was 310 acres and was expected to create 18,000 new jobs and 5,000 HKDL "cast members," which is Disney-speak for workers. HKDL was forecasted to bring in HK$19 billion over a forty-year plan. Notably officials projected 5.6 million yearly visitors.

Many Hong Kong students, scholars, activist groups, and community members believed that Disney had finagled the deal and questioned whether Hong Kong would reap any real economic benefits from the partnership. Complicating the matter, the negotiations that produced the agreement were nontransparent. Many of the details were revealed to the public through the media only when the deal was a fait accompli. When the public discovered that the HK SAR government had paid 90 percent of the fees and received

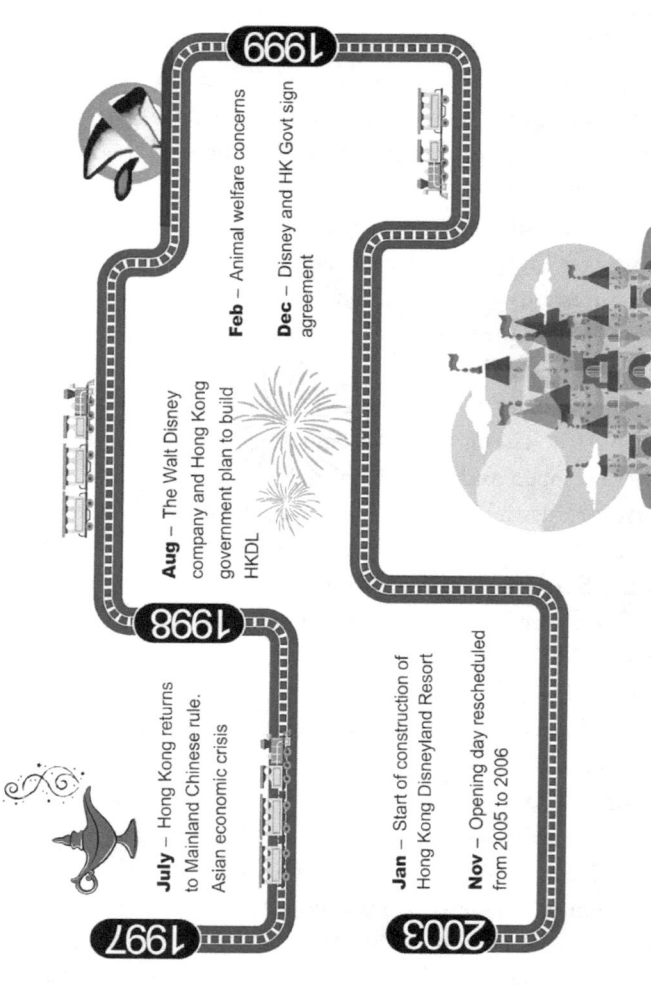

FIGURES 2–5. Hong Kong Disneyland timeline. (Credit: Allyssa Wu.)

2004

Aug – HKDL orders health inspectors to remove identifying caps causing bad publicity which forces Disney to apologize

Nov – $50 discount to HK residents to improve attendance which is unreleased

2005

Jan – 3 month open flexible admissions ticket causes holiday controversies

Sept 12 – HKDL Opening day: Pop stars, labor groups protests and former HKDL worker threatens suicide atop Space Mt

2006

Feb – Mainland Chinese go to park for Lunar New Year where tickets sell out and angry parents toss their children over the gates

June – HKDL decides not to serve shark fin soup amid environmental protests

2007

Animation Academy opens

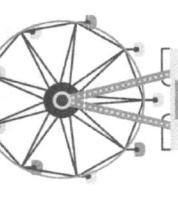

FIGURE 3

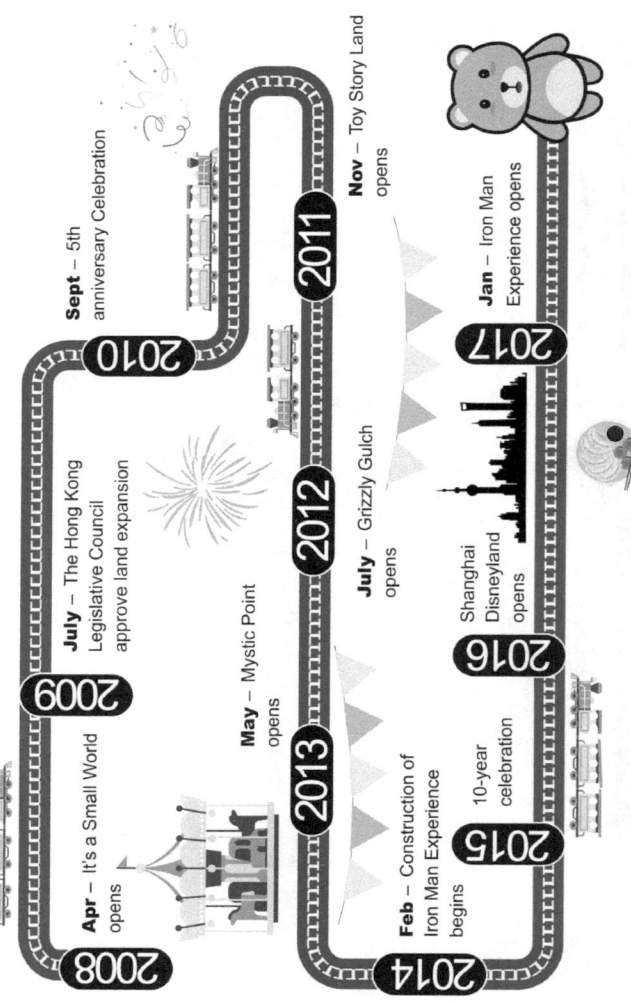

FIGURE 4

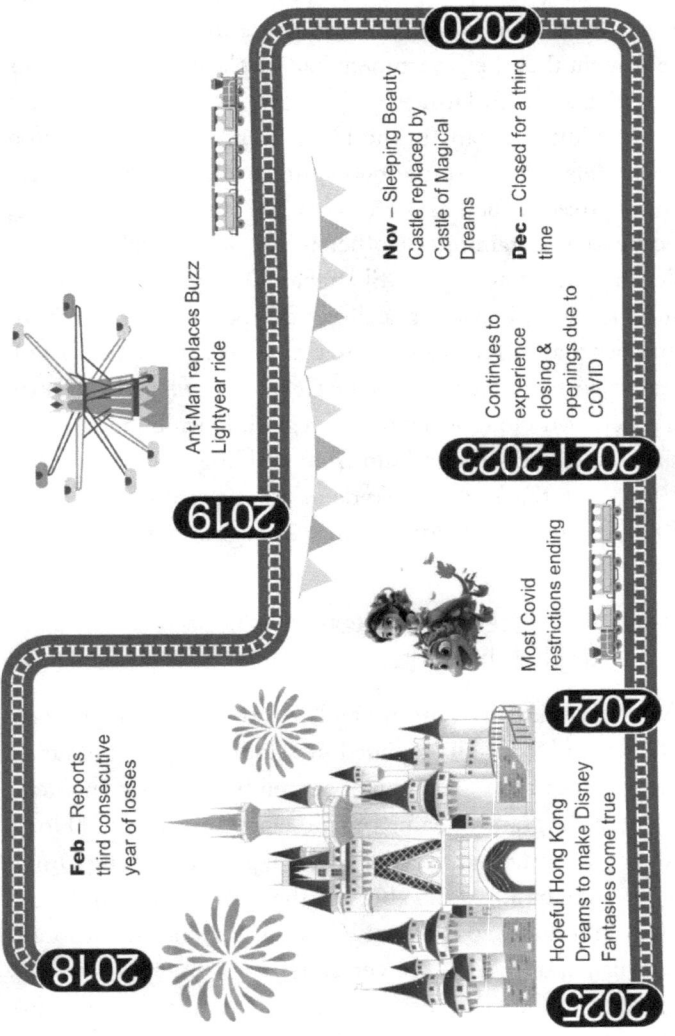

FIGURE 5

only 57 percent of the stakes, many locals were incensed. Despite newspaper articles that claimed that the majority of Hong Kongers approved of the project, many believed that the "mouse" had duped them (Frater 2005). There was also sentiment that the government had displayed weakness in its negotiations with Disney.

In addition, many in the Hong Kong community would have preferred to use the public funds spent on HKDL for other projects, such as more accessible low-income housing, occupational training, or other forms of local job creation. Adding insult to injury, Shanghai Disneyland opened on June 16, 2016, becoming a direct competitor that was both cheaper than HKDL and three times larger (Gaudiosi 2016). As a reporter wrote in the *South China Morning Post*, "Disney has betrayed Hong Kong in this regard. During initial negotiations, it pledged to refrain from building a second park in China. But that's what it has done" (Cheng 2016). HKDL, in short, has been controversial since its beginnings.

Opening Day, September 12, 2005: Suicide, Labor Protests, and Offended Pop Stars

After six years of planning and construction, Hong Kong Disneyland officially opened its doors to the public at one o'clock in the afternoon of September 12, 2005. In attendance at the grand opening ceremony were six hundred Hong Kong government officials, PRC vice president Zeng Qinghong, nine hundred members of the international and local press, and hundreds of local VIPs (local tycoons, corporate bigwigs, and stage and screen stars).

Despite the excitement, the event was marred by a number of troubling occurrences. Hong Kong governmental officials criticized the park. Local Cantopop stars such as Kelly Chen reported that they were mistreated and disrespected by

HKDL officials. Protestors gathered outside the park to draw attention to the alleged abuse of factory workers who supplied Disney merchandise (*CBS News* 2005). Local Hong Kongers were not impressed by the extremely small size of the park or the long lines for rides. There were also many allegations of labor abuse of the workers who built the park and those who worked in the park, as later chapters will discuss. Additionally, a former HKDL employee threatened to commit suicide on an attraction. In short, HKDL dealt with multiple public relations miscues from the day it opened.

When the deal was reached to create Hong Kong Disneyland, Hong Kong was struggling in multiple ways, and Disney was having difficulty making Disneyland Paris profitable. Because Hong Kong was in a precarious position economically and socially thanks to its return to mainland China in 1997, it fared worse than Disney in the negotiations. Hong Kong's residents were skeptical of the deal that produced the park, and despite considerable excitement, some of the public's criticisms affected the atmosphere on its opening day. Its troubles did not end there: although the park had been marketed as a panacea for Hong Kong's recent economic woes, with promises of an estimated 5.6 million visitors each year, HKDL did not achieve this initial projection. There was a forecast based on the assumption of ten million visitors a year after about five years (Frater 2005). It also experienced a significant drop in attendance after Shanghai Disneyland opened in 2016. From the beginning, Hong Kong Disneyland has been the site of negotiations and anxieties.

Methodology and Chapter Overview

This book is based on ethnographic field visits to Hong Kong from 2010 to 2012 and in 2014, 2016, 2018, 2023 and 2024.

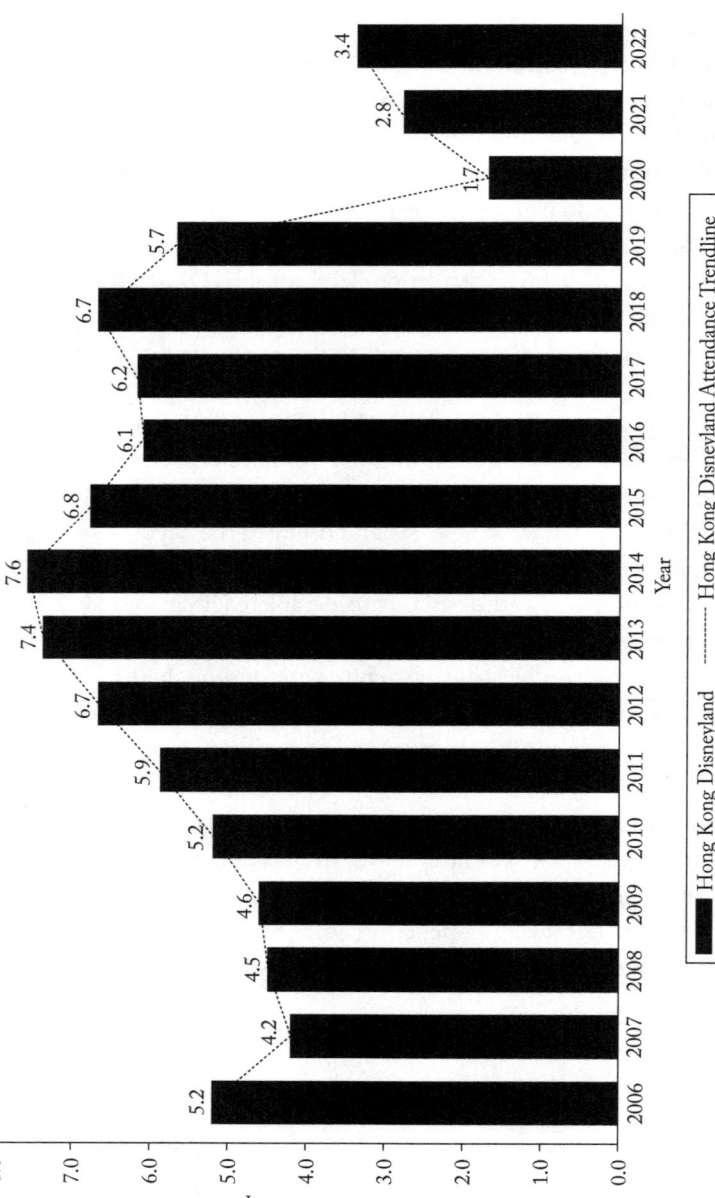

FIGURE 6. Hong Kong Disneyland attendance 2006–2022. Source: Hong Kong Disneyland (2009–2021). Note: HKDL closed in 2022 and intermittently closed in 2023. (Credit: Pedram Maymand.)

I performed participant observation and conducted surveys, archival research, oral histories, and formal and semiformal multihour interviews to construct a "thick description" of the site. The informants, all of them adults, represented a broad range of actors, including, on the HKDL company side, a marketer, an intermediary, and a manager, and, on the labor side, several HKDL workers and former workers and a union official. I also interviewed local residents and community activists in a variety of occupations.

Chapter 1 explains how unanticipated culture wars surrounding Hong Kong Disneyland have prevented the full indigenization of its consumer offerings. The developers made efforts to indigenize the culture, food, and marketing of the theme park to satisfy local visitors. Given that Hong Kong is a highly Westernized space that has adopted American products, these efforts at indigenization should have been successful. Ultimately, however, indigenization was a failure at HKDL because of the variety of demands for customized cultural, food, and marketing experiences, which led to reduced attendance at the park.

Chapter 2 discusses HKDL's labor practices. In pursuit of profit, HKDL tried to indigenize not only the space of the theme park but also its labor practices. The workers interviewed for this chapter expressed ambivalence about indigenization, citing negative public relations and adverse interactions with mainland Chinese tourists. HKDL's labor indigenization is complicated by factors that include perceptions of ethnic and national superiority, ambivalence, and continuing unequal treatment.

Chapter 3 discusses the spatial indigenization practices that Disney used in building HKDL. Disney's press releases claimed that the park was sensitive to cultural indigenization and hybridization because of the use of feng shui spatial practices. In reality, the attempts to use feng shui principles at the park are merely Orientalized performances, and few visitors notice or care about so-called space indigenization. Meanwhile, there is no dedicated space in HKDL that depicts Hong Kong's culture, history, or people.

To conclude this study, chapter 4 discusses HKDL's main local competitor: a theme park called Ocean Park. This chapter shows how, unlike HKDL, Ocean Park has successfully indigenized to the local Hong Kong population in terms of space, labor, and consumption.

1

Indigenizing Consumption

Culture Wars

My hair has puffed up to a ball of frizz, but I am happy as I make my way to the Winnie the Pooh ride. I see many mainland Chinese tourists and Hong Kong high school girls in line and reflect that this yellowish-orange and pleasantly plump Winnie the Pooh bear is one thing at Hong Kong Disneyland (HKDL) that mainland Chinese visitors will instantly recognize. I see a giant medieval scroll with English script that reads, "In which Pooh Begins His Search for Honey in a Very Enchanted Space. . . ." It occurs to me that many mainland Chinese visitors (who are the main tourists here) do not read or speak English well. I brace myself for the onslaught that is about to occur.

3 . . . 2 . . . 1 . . .

"Hey! Stay in your place!" an angry Hong Kong middle-aged man screams at a mainland Chinese boy in Cantonese, knowing full well that he is unlikely to understand the dialect. I can feel the anger of the Hong Kong locals as they become agitated at the mainland Chinese tourists trying to cut in line; I am told by an HKDL worker there is a screaming fight here every day. A lone mainland Chinese teenage boy slowly

and sneakily moves himself up and through the queue. His queue-jumping skills seem finely honed, and I notice that he has cut past at least five or six people. He slowly looks up and around at a distance to avoid suspicion. Sometimes he makes stealthy Jenga-like moves, quickly turning right or left into an open pocket; at other times he charges forward, giving the impression he has someplace to go. He pretends that he does not hear or understand the angry grumblings of the Hong Kongers, who were line-trained by McDonald's in the 1970s. A frazzled young HKDL staff member is at the top of the line speaking in Cantonese with a Mandarin accent, imploring guests to hold their positions in the line—a message clearly directed at mainland Chinese line-cutters. An overhead speaker also reminds people not to jump the queue.

The next thing I see is a group of five Hong Kong schoolgirls in white uniforms with blue ties who have linked their arms, with one girl at each end holding on to the side of the railing. These determined teenagers have spread their feet and arms to make a human chain that nobody can penetrate. With their arms and legs spread, these Hong Kong schoolgirls successfully foil the efforts of the mainland Chinese teenager to cut the line any further; he's defeated. I am embarrassed to admit this now, but my family followed suit and we also linked our arms to the railings to prevent line-cutters.

This vignette gives a snapshot of the culture war between mainland Chinese tourists and Hong Kong locals. Mainland Chinese tourists often do not accept standing in line, not out of poor manners but because there is no queuing culture in mainland China. Indeed, people did not stand in line in Hong Kong until they were trained to so at locations of McDonald's, which opened its first Hong Kong branch in 1975 (Watson 1997). One of my HKDL worker interviewees noted that Hong Kong's status as a former British colony

DRAWING 2. Hong Kong schoolgirls holding their ground. (Credit: Sally Pirie.)

generates arguments over the Western "civilizing mission" between Hong Kong locals and mainland Chinese tourists every day. Although the civilizing mission was purportedly an attempt to improve an ethnic group through the inculcation of Western cultural norms, it has in reality served as a justification for imperialism or colonialism. In this case, however, the "civilizers" are colonialized Hong Kong British subjects and the "mission" is aimed at mainland Chinese. These arguments often involve screaming, pointing, and yelling. In addition to the frustrations over queue-jumping, I have seen Hong Kong locals yell at mainland Chinese children and adults for public urination, squatting, and spitting.

The presence of these disputes between different Chinese cultures is one of the many reasons it is impossible to fully indigenize consumption at HKDL. In particular, queue-jumping is an issue that the U.S.-based Walt Disney Company did not anticipate. Ultimately, the reduced attendance rates of the park indicate that the indigenization efforts of the developers failed. HKDL was projected to attract over five million people annually when it first opened, but actual attendance was much lower; in fact, Disney refused to

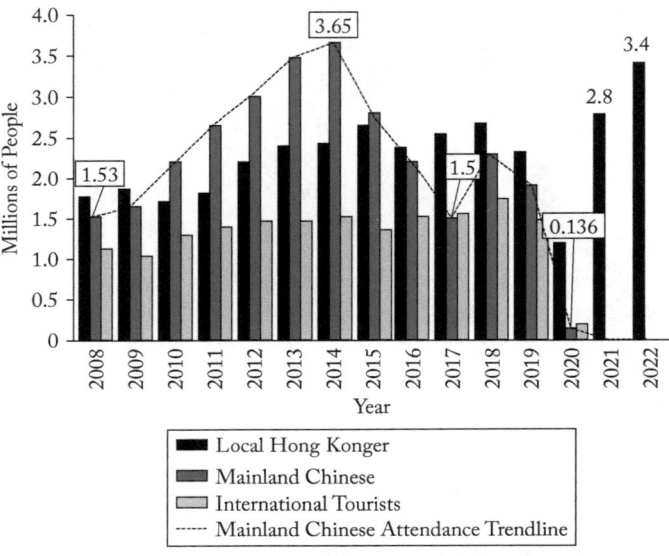

FIGURE 7. Hong Kong Disneyland attendance 2008–2022: Local Hong Konger, mainland Chinese, and international. Source: Hong Kong Disneyland (2009–2023). (Credit: Pedram Maymand.)

release attendance figures of the park for two years even though the facility is partly owned by the Hong Kong government. One way of measuring human action is by participation or nonparticipation, or what is known as "voting with your feet." Attendance is also a form of cultural practice, and figure 7 shows the different attendance trends for Hong Kong locals, mainland Chinese tourists, and international tourists. This chapter argues that the developers of HKDL attempted to indigenize in the areas of culture, food, and marketing, especially by providing trilingual signs and recruiting trilingual employees. Given that Hong Kong is a highly Westernized space, Disney's indigenization strategies should have been successful. Three key reasons for its failure are presented below: the diverse needs of local and mainland visitors, the unanticipated culture wars between these two groups, and an inability to compete with local food offerings.

Cultural Indigenization

Disney made attempts to appeal to local tastes in setting up HKDL. One important step was the recruitment of trilingual staff. Many front-stage HKDL workers can switch easily between English, Cantonese, and Mandarin for the convenience of their visitors. This shows that Disney understood that the park would have three main types of clientele: Hong Kong locals, mainland Chinese tourists, and international tourists. Hong Kong locals speak Cantonese, as does much of the Chinese diaspora in Southeast Asia and the Americas. Many Cantonese speakers, especially from Hong Kong, Taiwan, and Southeast Asia, can also speak Mandarin, albeit with an accent that is different from that of mainland Chinese. Although a multitude of dialects are spoken in mainland China, Mandarin or Pǔtōnghuà (普通話; 普通话) is the lingua franca. Meanwhile, English is provided for visitors from outside China and the Chinese diaspora, on the basis that most international tourists are able to speak and understand English.

It is a further credit to Disney's cultural competence that the company understood the need for English, simplified Chinese, and traditional Chinese signage throughout the park. All signs for rides, guideposts, maps, and directions are in English and in both types of Chinese characters. This decision reflects the use of traditional Chinese characters (漢語) in Hong Kong and simplified Chinese (汉语) in mainland China, where a simplified script has been adopted to increase literacy rates among the population. For the Jungle River Cruise, for example, there are two or three lines to join depending on which language a visitor prefers.

Depending on the line a visitor joins, the skipper will tell his corny jokes in English, Cantonese, or Mandarin.

Another good example of HKDL's successful accommodation of guests is its Broadway-style show "The Festival of the Lion King," which uses live singers and dancers alongside large puppets to celebrate the classic Disney animated film *The Lion King* (1994). This large-scale production is seamlessly narrated in both Cantonese and English, with simplified Chinese surtitles appearing on a monitor for Mandarin Chinese tourists. This approach makes the show accessible and friendly to visitors who are comfortable with any of English, Cantonese, or Mandarin.

HKDL was always intended to attract mostly mainland Chinese and international tourists (Choi 2012). Executives were aware that operating the park for local Hong Kong visitors alone would not be profitable. One interviewee described the attendance as extremely low and argued that Disney was full of hubris in its projections over five million visitors. The attendance figures indicate cultural elements of HKDL's failure. Culture is a reflection of human activity, and in the HKDL case, deciding whether to visit the park is partly a cultural act of voting with one's feet. Choosing not to visit the park can also be seen as an indicator of resistance to or rejection of its presence. Attendance figures can therefore be used as evidence for cultural decision making.

The annual number of local Hong Kong visitors has been relatively steady, in the range of 1.7 to 2.6 million. In 2008, around 1.8 million Hong Kong locals visited HKDL, which made them the largest group of visitors. In the following year, the number rose to 1.88 million. After a drop in attendance in 2010, there was a steady increase every year until 2015, and the numbers continued to increase even after Shanghai Disneyland opened in 2016. Yet attendance dropped sharply with the outbreak of COVID-19, which forced the park to close for extended periods. The annual number of international visitors was also consistent until the pandemic halted international travel.

In contrast, there is a clear trend of ascent and decline in the number of mainland Chinese visitors. In 2008, there were around 1.53 million visitors from mainland China, with a steady and sometimes sharp increase in attendance every year through to 2015. From 2009 to 2010, the number of visitors from mainland China increased from 1.65 million to 2.2 million, and in 2014 the numbers peaked at 3.65 million. In 2015 there were almost a million fewer visitors from mainland China, and after Shanghai Disneyland opened in 2016, it seems likely that many chose to go there instead of traveling to Hong Kong. Only in 2018 did the number of mainland Chinese visitors start to recover, but the outbreak of COVID-19 led to closures at the border and of HKDL.

There are many possible ways to explain why fewer mainland Chinese have been visiting HKDL. The decrease in visitor numbers from mainland China after 2014 might be related to the Umbrella Movement or the Occupy Movement in Hong Kong from September 26 to December 15, 2014, a protest against the enforcement of mainland Chinese laws in Hong Kong. There was international coverage of sit-ins and occupations of buildings, and images in the media showed police officers clashing with Hong Kong protestors. Protests against the 2020 National Security Law from mainland China have also erupted. One might surmise that people in mainland China are reluctant to visit a place where televised clashes between Hong Kong protesters and law enforcement occurred.

Food and Space Indigenization

Attempts were made at HKDL to indigenize food menus to local tastes by offering Disney-themed Hong Kong delicacies. For example, the park serves a *Toy Story*–themed dim sum, with the food shaped into aliens and pigs from the film. Dim sum, which has long been popular in Hong Kong as brunch, consists of many small items for a family to share. HKDL also offers popular Hong Kong drinks and desserts based on Disney characters. A green slushie is called the Musician: a summer drink featuring Olu Mel, a friendly sea turtle with a ukulele from the Duffy and Friends line of merchandise. Colorful *Toy Story*–themed desserts are based on common sweets found throughout Hong Kong: a Buzz Lightyear panna cotta, Lotso banana cake, and Rex lemon honey cake.

There has also been a sincere attempt at HKDL to use beloved local Chinese recipes in its high-level hotel restaurants. The Hong Kong Disneyland Hotel has a good reputation, and its restaurant is advertised as award-winning. Its menu features Sichuan, Beijing, Shanghai, and Guangdong specialty dishes, which are found in Hong Kong restaurants. One such dish is wok-fried Wagyu beef cubes with mango and avocado sauce, which in the Disneyland Hotel comes with appetizing sides shaped like Mickey Mouse's ears.

Hong Kong is known for its gastronomic excellence, and Cantonese food is highly regarded around the world. As shown in figure 7, HKDL does try to sell Cantonese food, but with mixed results. It is not easy to match popular Hong Kong food on price or quality. For example, the roasted pit beef wrap, roasted pit chicken wrap, and turkey legs, at HK$20, HK$20, and HK$30, respectively, are uninspiring and much more expensive than their equivalents outside the gates. Likewise, the curried fish balls (HK$10) and hot dogs (HK$15) are sold for significantly more than street prices. At these price points, the Disney food offerings are unlikely to be successful in comparison to the local street food, especially because the typical Hong Kong local is financially savvy and can easily recognize the price difference.

Another failure in HKDL's attempts to indigenize the food offerings at the park, and also perhaps in its marketing, has been its handling of controversial shark fin soup. According to Chinese and Hong Kong wedding traditions, it is common to serve shark fin soup to display wealth and prosperity. Although this practice would not be accepted in other cultural contexts, HKDL planned to offer shark fin soup to attract wedding celebrations, from which park executives believed they would earn significant revenue. However, this decision put HKDL's indigenizing message in the crosshairs of animal rights activists, such as Sea Shepherd.[1] To reduce controversy, shark fin soup was removed from menus at HKDL and mentioned only in a pamphlet as a dish that would be provided on request. Hong Kong activists disagreed with this decision, and there was negative coverage of HKDL in the Western and Hong Kong media. As the practice of shark finning became more widely known, environmentalists and parkgoers questioned the decision of HKDL to offer the soup. One group of protestors even came to HKDL dressed as bloody sharks. The operators of HKDL surrendered and chose not to provide the park's visitors with the traditional Chinese wedding dish. By the time shark fin soup was removed from menus, however, the association of HKDL with the controversial practice of shark finning had already placed a dark cloud over the park.

In 2005, many of the food options that were available at the park were designed with tourists rather than local Hong Kongers in mind. Hong Kong has rich local culinary traditions that are inexpensive. At HKDL the food was very expensive but also shaped in a way that was not palpable to the locals. One could argue that HKDL went through a process of "self-Orientalization" in which Disney's park planners have shaped the menu into an Orientalist fantasy, which is often done in Chinese restaurants in the United States.

The architecture of the wishing well, with its upturned eaves and roof corners, is an example of space indigenization. Philip Choy reports in *The Architecture of San Francisco's Chinatown* (2012) that Euro-American architects were hired to create "authentic" Chinese false-front buildings as a means of survival for the Chinese American community. Throughout HKDL there are many Asian elements that are employed, such as feng shui spatial elements. The number four is not in elevators, as it sounds like death in Cantonese. This makes for an "immersive" experience for foreign tourists but does not impress locals or inspire them to pay for food that offers such an experience. Ultimately, HKDL's food and space indigenization falls short and can be considered a disappointment.

Marketing Indigenization

Seeking to avoid some of the cultural miscues of other Disneyland developments, HKDL also tried to indigenize its marketing to appeal to Hong Kong locals in multiple ways. The developers extensively studied local community needs by holding focus groups and administering mass surveys about wants and needs. Disney researched the local knowledge of Disney characters and products and found that it was not as robust in Hong Kong as in the United States (oral history, tourism expert, 2008). One HKDL middle manager told me that mass surveys had revealed that the guests were 40 percent mainland Chinese tourists, 30 percent Southeast Asian tourists, and 30 percent Hong Kong locals. The mass surveys revealed when different visitors took their holidays and the types of food they preferred. An HKDL executive stated, "We learn things by listening, such as food preferences. By the fifth year of operation, we noticed trends: a market that is twice as large in spring as in autumn, with many more Indian guests. We learned their school holiday times. We then needed to brief our park staff and rethink. We have to make sure that everyone knows where the Indian food is; everyone must know and we need to continually plan that" (interview 2012).

The executives learned a lot about the travel plans of Indian and mainland Chinese visitors from these questionnaires. In response to an increase in guests from India, owing to Hong Kong's relative proximity, the HKDL hotels added more vegetarian food to their menus. The surveys also revealed the intensity of mainland Chinese travel in February during the period of the Lunar or Chinese New Year. One HKDL executive reported, "This is when China closes down for ten days and generally people head home." He estimated that 60 to 70 percent of all Hong Kong tourists from mainland China visited HKDL during this brief period each year (interview 2012).

Roy Tan Hardy, vice president of marketing and sales of HKDL, has stated that extensive surveys of Hong Kong residents indicated that they preferred the classic Disneyland in Anaheim, which is smaller than Disney World in Orlando, Florida, Tokyo Disneyland, and Disneyland Paris (formerly Euro Disney). Disney began its push to market HKDL to the Hong Kong community via many avenues in 2003. For example, director of marketing Jennifer Chua pointed to the placement of Disney television programming on the TVB Jade channel (Dembina 2005). Animated shows and three mini documentaries on the history of Disney theme parks were also used to educate Hong Kong people about the Disney brand.

HKDL has a community relations specialist tasked with reaching out to the local community. For example, the specialist is responsible for managing Disney VoluntEARS, the company's volunteering program. The community relations specialist organizes a series of community activities with the participation of staff from a broad range of Disney's business units. I corresponded with a former HKDL community relations specialist about his duties via email. He replied that the theme park had "stakeholder engagement with non-governmental organizations (NGOs), community and charitable groups" (email response survey, July 18, 2013). The park's operators were diligent in trying to involve community groups by giving away free tickets and offering presentations. He also pointed to the liaison work done with the Disney Worldwide Outreach team to launch various global initiatives locally. Of the community outreach employees I interviewed, this former community relations specialist was the only one who seemed attracted to the Disney brand and saw its efforts as successful: "The community work that Hong Kong Disneyland did [was] quite successful. Through our VoluntEARS, we were able to provide the 'Disney magic' to those who were in need, such as some special in-park activities like 'Disney's Magical Christmas'" (email response survey, July 18, 2013).

This specialist further noted that the park used community engagement work to establish and maintain rapport with local NGOs and community and charitable organizations. Key programs include the territory-wide Jiminy Cricket's Environmentality Challenge, which involves primary school students making an environmental pledge and participating in group projects. The program aims to help raise environmental awareness among young students. The theme park operators also arrange regular hospital visits by VoluntEARS and Disney ambassadors. The former

Disney community outreach employee indicated that all Hong Kong Disneyland cast members were welcome to join the community engagement work organized by the community relations team, at which point "they would then become Disney VoluntEARS" (email response survey, July 18, 2013).

The former Disney community outreach employee reported that the community relations team engaged with various NGOs and community groups across Hong Kong through various programs in three specific areas: community, children, and the environment. The theme park also began to develop rapport within neighboring communities, such as the Tung Chung area. For example, the park directly engaged with local service groups, including the Boys' and Girls' Clubs Association of Hong Kong and Po Leung Kuk, by giving tickets away. The purpose of these programs and initiatives was to establish and maintain a strong rapport with the NGOs, to build trust, and to strengthen the relationships between HKDL and various community entities. From the perspective of this former employee, these initiatives were quite successful as marketing strategies and tactics; nonetheless, none of my other informants had heard about any of these community endeavors.

HKDL is heavily marketed on social media in mainland China and Hong Kong. Digital marketing on social media platforms, such as Facebook and YouTube, has increased as the park has sought to woo local Hong Kong young adults to visit. Questionnaires helped to reveal the locals' love of Christmas, and when the marketing department noticed increasing numbers of Hong Kong young adults coming to the park specifically for its Christmas attractions, it responded by putting up more Christmas decorations and expanding Christmas promotions. For example, commercials were aired highlighting the "winter wonderland" elements of the park, and brochures showed Mickey and Minnie in winter clothes in front of a nicely decorated Christmas tree.

Despite these efforts, there have been multiple public relations and marketing issues that HKDL did not anticipate or address in a timely matter. In general, many of my informants commented that the marketing and public relations were very poor. One interviewee said the Disney marketers came in the morning and were fired by the afternoon (oral history, HKDL negotiator, 2008). Although this might be an exaggeration, it is true that many staff members of the HKDL marketing department were dismissed from their jobs.

In 2006 there was a major negative public relations and marketing debacle over ticketing for Chinese New Year. The tickets being sold by HKDL could be redeemed anytime within six months of purchase. When huge numbers of mainland Chinese ticket holders tried to redeem their tickets during the Lunar New Year period, the park exceeded its capacity and staff had to refuse entry to hundreds of tourists. Some visitors with valid tickets were turned away at the gates, some tried to scale the park walls to enter, and others tried to pass their children over the Disney gates to the other side. Many Hong Kong locals also expressed anger, screaming, "That is not how to do business properly." Images of these disgruntled locals and tourists were broadcast all over the world, dealing a major blow to the park's public relations efforts. Bill Ernest, then HKDL's executive vice president and managing director, tried to minimize the damage at a press conference with an apology. Nonetheless, HKDL was slow to react to the media reports of people trying to sneak into the park. News travels fast in Hong Kong, and people expect problems to be addressed rapidly. In the days between the ticket riots and HKDL's explanation of what had happened, people in Hong Kong developed negative views of the park and its operators.

The violent prodemocracy and anti–extradition bill protests in Hong Kong in 2019 and 2020, which were among the largest protests in Hong Kong's history, had a negative effect on tourism, although they were beyond Disney's control (Russolillo and Xie 2019). These protests followed the 2014 Umbrella Movement and were broadcast all over the world, and they might have led some tourists to decide not to visit Hong Kong. The drop in overall tourist numbers affected attendance at HKDL during these periods of unrest.

Indigenization Failures: An Analysis

I opened this chapter with a vignette illustrating three key reasons for the failure of HKDL indigenization, one of which is the cultural friction over queuing. At the park there is a distinct mismatch in "manners" in regard to how one should stand in line. It is not uncommon to hear Hong Kong residents make fun of "the ugly mainlander," who is seen as uncouth and criticized for using "new money" to buy up million-dollar properties in Hong Kong. The perception that HKDL is targeting mainland Chinese tourists makes it unappealing to some Hong Kong residents. As one of my local Hong Kong businessman informants put it, "Hong Kong Disneyland is not organized; the queuing, pushing around—very rude. [Anaheim Disneyland] is friendly. The mainland Chinese people—they push—spitting, yelling, spitting. Aiming at the mainland Chinese—that is the worst thing about the park" (oral history, Hong Kong businessman, 2010). One can perceive a sort of racist sentiment from local Hong Kong people toward mainland Chinese tourists.

Indeed, every time my family and I went to HKDL we observed a shouting match between a local Hong Kong resident and a mainland Chinese child or adult. Furthermore, many of the interviewed workers reported that there were daily verbal fights at the park, making the reality a long way from the slogan describing Disney parks as the "happiest place on earth." One day I observed a Hong Kong mother screaming in Cantonese at a mainland Chinese child who had cut in front of her and her family. The child did not understand Cantonese and was surprised and confused by the woman's reaction. Both parties in this conflict acted appropriately given their respective cultural scripts: the mother's intense reaction was undoubtedly fueled by a genuine belief that the child's line-cutting was inappropriate, whereas the child's surprise clearly indicated his lack of understanding of why it would be considered inappropriate.

In fact, as mentioned above, China lacks a culture of queuing, whereas most people in Hong Kong follow Western queuing norms. The British are famously "orderly" in their willingness to wait in line, and Hong Kongers might have picked up some of this habit when Hong Kong was a British colony or from their visits to McDonald's (Watson 1997). In many countries around the world, however, it is normal and natural to jockey ahead and cut lines to get to the front. This is the case in mainland China.

Citing Rongrong Zhou, an assistant professor of marketing at Hong Kong University of Science and Technology, a reporter for the *New York Times* writes that the differences go beyond a Hong Kong–mainland split. Zhou, who has studied the psychology of queuing in Hong Kong, although not at theme parks, has found that there is a tendency among Asians and others in more collective cultures to compare their situation with those around them. This may make it more likely that they will remain in a line even if it is excessively long (Fountain 2005). Zhou finds that in some cultures it is the people behind who determine the behavior of the one in front, as people do not want to give their position to others behind them. "In contrast," she states, "Americans and others in more individualistic societies make fewer 'social comparisons' of this sort. They don't necessarily feel better that more people are behind them, but feel bad if too many people are in front of them. Lines in these cultures tend to be more self-limiting" (Fountain 2005).

But the tension between mainland Chinese and Hong Kong locals goes well beyond queuing habits. There have been many recent notable instances of disputes between mainland Chinese and Hong Kong residents in Hong Kong. In one viral social media video, a Hong Kong man berates a fifteen-year-old mainland Chinese girl for eating on the MTR (Ko 2012), using what might be called "civilizing mission" tactics. Some Hong Kongers feel that mainlanders are acting like uncouth country bumpkins when they spit, talk at a high volume, or squat publicly. In response to the video, a Peking University professor, Kong Qingdong, was quoted as saying, "Some Hong Kong people don't see themselves as Chinese.... They are bastards," before adding, "These people are too used to being running dogs for British imperialists" (Ko 2012).

Such attitudes can be partly explained by Hong Kongers' fear of being overrun by the mainland Chinese. In the midst of a massive shortage of housing and some goods, Hong Kongers see wealthy mainland Chinese buying out fancy department store goods and purchasing lavish apartments. In *Anthropology News*, Sara Bergstresser recounts seeing mainland Chinese buying suitcases full of baby formula at a time when there was a formula shortage in Hong Kong: "The baby milk was not being bought by new parents; rather, it was being purchased by shoppers from mainland China to transport over the border and resell for profit" (Bergstresser 2022). This made Hong Kong parents understandably angry. There is also a shortage of hospital beds for Hong Kong women giving birth, and mainland Chinese women are accused of sneaking into Hong Kong and giving birth so that their babies may achieve Hong Kong residency. In 2019, Audrey Li wrote in the *South China Morning Post* that "Hong Kong's hatred of mainlanders [was feeding] the xenophobic undercurrents of its protests" over the hate crimes that were directed to mainland Chinese. "Incidents such as these," she continued, "shed light on a more complicated, less-covered side of the months-long protests: the deep distrust and even hatred towards mainland Chinese as a whole, while the movement has largely been viewed by the world as just a fight between democracy and authoritarianism" (Li 2019). In reaction to this complex culture war, Hong Kong identity has increasingly turned inward, incorporating a decreasing sense of Chinese personhood. When asked how they identified themselves, the majority of my interviewees stated that they were "Hong Kongers," not "Chinese."

In another *SCMP* article, journalist Amy Li tries to answer the question, "Why Are Chinese Tourists so Rude?" Li proposes that they lack global etiquette education and that they simply follow the rules of where they are from. For example, there is no tipping in China. Li also notes that some Chinese do not even follow local Chinese laws because they see their leaders disregarding the law: "Living in China, where the rule-of-law doesn't exist, means everyone has to look out for their own interest. It means people have little or no respect for laws" (Li 2016). The effects of over a hundred years of British colonialization on the public behavior of the Hong Kong populace are felt here. It is not safe for people in Hong Kong to publicly protest the Beijing government, so they instead lash out at mainland Chinese tourists. This is a plausible explanation for some of the violent verbal disputes I overheard at HKDL. The culture war directly relates to the marketing of the park because of the perception that it was developed for mainland Chinese tourists. Some Hong Kong residents are likely to avoid HKDL if they expect to encounter large numbers of mainland Chinese tourists.

The food served at HKDL is an odd mix of Western and ostensibly Cantonese dishes, albeit using recipes that often differ from the non-Disney versions in some significant ways. As one Hong Kong Disney executive told me, "The greatest issue, honestly, they have claimed they are culturally relevant when they arrived and they studied [local cuisine]. They studied everything and they introduced very simplified Westernized Chinese food on opening [day]. They had Western BBQ rice and Hainanese chicken rice and they had a Western chef and a Western staff dominated. They claimed they are local but guests knew" (interview, Hong Kong high executive). Similarly, attempts to import variations of typical American food have also missed the mark. I observed one Anglo-American enter the Main Street bakery and gruffly object to the interpretation of pie: "These are not pies, where are the pies?" The worker repeatedly pointed to a sinicized fruit pie, which was more akin to a tart and filled with solid egg custard instead of fruit. Hong Kong "pies" are Chinese versions of American pies; they are doughier, contain little fruit, and are not overly sweet. They would be unrecognizable to an American in search of a classic American pie.

One could argue, however, that HKDL was attempting to adjust to local tastes by offering a Chinese interpretation of pie. For example, when Krispy Kreme came to Hong Kong, the company was expected to be as profitable as KFC, Pizza Hut, and McDonald's but soon went out of business because its executives underestimated the degree to which the people of Hong Kong tend to eschew both overly sweet items, such as Western-style pies and cakes, and dairy-based dessert items (Anderson 1988). The lack of intensely sweet food means that the food experience at HKDL is different from that at its American counterparts. Funnel cakes, for instance, are a staple item at Anaheim Disneyland but are nowhere to be seen at HKDL. Visitors who are used to the typical American theme park fare of fried and sugary items may be dissatisfied with the food on offer.

Despite the indigenization efforts, however, HKDL's food hardly seems to satisfy the locals. Many Hong Kong locals have to search for nostalgic foods along with international cuisines. In *Hong Kong Foodways*, Sidney Cheung writes, "If I had to name a comfort food, I would say claypot rice, with steamed chicken /pork ribs and Chinese sausage and Cantonese congee with preserved duck egg and lean pork meat. Both can be found everywhere in Hong Kong" (Cheung 2022, 55). These items are not found in HKDL. The street food in Hong Kong is delicious and inexpensive, and many locals choose to pay less than US$2 at the local street stall rather than cooking for themselves. A Cantonese meal that rivals that of a Michelin star restaurant is available right on the street or maybe in the eighth-floor food court of an unassuming building. Hong Kong cuisine is economical, earnest, and electrifyingly evocative: to quote Anthony Bourdain, "Cheap delicious food served from open-air stalls. Pull up a plastic stool. Crack a beer. Fire up the wok" (Cho 2018).

As with other forms of consumption, food consumption traditions are not created in a vacuum. In *Distinction: A Social Critique of the Judgment of Taste*, Pierre Bourdieu (1984) famously argued that what and where people eat is a marker of their class or cultural capital. As a Western product, Disneyland might seem to confer a higher status on Hong Kong; after all, it is a marker of class for a resident of Hong Kong to purchase a foreign product from Europe, Japan, or the United States. However, this might not be the case for HKDL. One of my local interviewees asked, "Why can't Hong Kong have its own Hong Kong attractions and not import Western ones?" (oral history 2010). Similar complaints were aired in other interviews. Especially since 1997, Hong Kong has competed economically and culturally with mainland Chinese cities, such as Shanghai, and other Asian countries, such as Singapore, Thailand, Korea, and Japan. In the case of Disney, some of my interviewees were very proud to tell me that they did not go to HKDL, and it was clear that they felt superior to those who visited the park. This appears to be a case of invoking a sense of possessing greater cultural capital than the mainland Chinese visitors, even if the latter might be wealthier.

The rich street food tradition in Hong Kong gives HKDL a high bar to clear in its food offerings. Hong Kong locals often complained that the food at the park was too expensive, peculiar (in looks, form, and taste), and culturally insensitive. A teenage interviewee expressed disgust at her US$10 BBQ rice and said she could get the "real deal" at less than half the price and with double the flavor four MTR stops away. In fact, the food at Disneyland was perceived by Hong Kong residents as unsuccessful in a myriad of ways. A good example of HKDL's problematic food choices and presentation is its choice to sell food items (e.g., hot dogs and squid sticks) wrapped in plastic, something one would never see in the United States or on Hong Kong streets.

In examining HKDL's food offerings, it is important to problematize the notion of "authentic" Chinese food. Margery Fee argues in "Who Can Write as Other?" (1995) that demands for authenticity deny Fourth World writers a living, changing culture (243). To extend this analysis to the consumption of food, we must interrogate the notion of authentic Chinese food. Chinese food has continually changed over the centuries and has always been influenced by China's geography (see Coe 2009). Hong Kong imports many of its food supplies from overseas, particularly from mainland China. Many Chinese food experts argue that what we often think of as authentic Chinese food is actually Chinese cuisine that has been improvised outside China (Anderson 1988; Coe 2009; Lee 2008; Wu and Cheung 2002). Among the plethora of examples of the adaptation of Chinese food to foreign countries are Chinese American, Chinese Italian, and Chinese Caribbean food. Hong Kong is also charged with being an inauthentically Chinese space because of its long history of British colonialism. Crafting a menu that can meet the diverse expectations of Hong Kong, mainland Chinese, and international appetites is therefore a real difficulty for the operators of HKDL.

Furthermore, Sidney Cheung contends that the "local" in Hong Kong food culture is actually quite global: "When Hong Kong people dine out they seek variety and a wide range of choices. Perhaps eating in McDonald's for breakfast, lunching at a Japanese restaurant, buying snacks at the Taiwan tea shop, and having Indian curry for dinner. . . . All of these kinds of foods are found in Hong Kong" (Wu and Cheung 2002, 110). The identity of which this food culture forms a part is, as Stuart Hall (1990) reminds us, linked to concepts of the local but is not static; rather, local identity is always in a state of becoming. Wu and Cheung (2002) argue that China has fewer food taboos than many other cultures because it has suffered and survived many famines. This may lead some to conclude that Chinese food is not held to the same standards as other cuisines, but it also makes food central to the culture. Sidney Mintz observes that it is "seriously misleading to deemphasize the importance of food in Han Culture" (quoted in Wu and Cheung 2002, xvii). Disney, it seems, might not have understood the critical importance of food to some of the park's most valuable patrons.

The marketing of HKDL has been difficult because of issues outside the control of its operators. Before the COVID-19 outbreak of 2020, the image of Hong Kong

Island had already been transformed from a site of "East-West playground" into a site of "terror and death." Nonetheless, many of my informants commented that the marketing and public relations of the park were very poor. Some of the marketing failures were related to a misreading of the target market. One journalist and Disney theorist I interviewed in 2023 stated that Disneyland in Hong Kong was not as effective as it could have been given Disney's success as a corporation. Disneyland has survived and grown for over fifty years and even expanded its brand globally, but it might have met its match in trying to appeal to all Hong Kong locals and mainland Chinese tourists. The journalist believed that Disney had tried to recognize the differences between these groups, and between each of them and other audiences, but that it had ultimately misunderstood its target market. The journalist observed that Disney must not overestimate the cultural differences between Asian visitors and others (interview 2010). Disney's market research indicated that Asians like to take photographs. Accordingly, HKDL's planners designed the park with a number of scenic spots for photo opportunities. Addressing the local penchant for taking photos from every possible angle has been harder: one step has been to install an additional stationary teacup next to the line for the Mad Hatter teacups ride so that visitors can take photos while they wait without slowing down the loading and unloading process of the ride. However, as discussed earlier, the park has failed to offer an adequate number of exhilarating attractions and major shows to keep visitors occupied for a whole day. Many of my local Hong Kong interviewees mentioned that the park is too small and lacks the thrilling rides that are available at Ocean Park. As the journalist told me, "We like to play with the camera relative to Americans, Europeans, but we also like thrilling rides and watching shows. So I think they made the mistake [of thinking it was] either/or... and not both" (interview 2010). The park's designers relied on their market research in trying to meet the local demand for photo opportunities, but they neglected to provide other key aspects of a theme park, such as a variety of thrilling rides and attractions.

Meanwhile, the differences between visitors from Hong Kong and from mainland China might have been underestimated. Time and again in my interviews locals expressed their belief that the park was intended for mainland Chinese and international tourists. One Hong Kong educator indicated that compared to Ocean Park, HKDL did not have enough features related to Hong Kong. However, this view was not universal: another Hong Kong businessman said that he wished the park were more global, like Disney World in Orlando. Many of my Hong Kong resident respondents knew that a large percentage (over 30 percent) of HKDL visitors were mainland Chinese tourists, and most acknowledged that Hong Kong needed tourists to support its economy. After 1997, many long-distance tourists ceased coming to Hong Kong, and it was important to the tourism industry that they be replaced by mainland Chinese visitors. Indeed, the park was sold to local people on the basis that it would bring in more global tourists. The belief held by some Hong Kong residents that HKDL was built specifically to bring in more mainland Chinese tourists is problematic on many levels and feeds into the distrust that many Hong Kong residents feel toward mainland China.

Most importantly, the notion that mainland Chinese visitors would flock to HKDL fails to recognize that the population of mainland China, especially adults and the elderly, has had little direct contact with Disney products. In China, there are many theme parks and neighborhoods that "mimic" other places around the globe (Bosker 2013), and these include Disney-like theme parks that appropriate Disney characters without authorization. However, when I asked one interviewee in his sixties whether he knew a lot about Disney, he responded that he knew little: Disney was not of his generation, and his own children preferred Harry Potter and Korean and Japanese popular culture.

Furthermore, Hong Kong maintains tight restrictions on access to the island for people from mainland China who wish to visit as tourists or settle as long-term residents. Visas can be difficult for people from mainland China to obtain. In this context, one of my interviewees considered the marketing of HKDL as consisting of cheap gimmicks for attracting mainland Chinese tourists. For example, he noted that the park offered a special one-day visa that allowed mainland Chinese to enter Hong Kong only to visit HKDL, after which they must return immediately to the mainland. My interviewee, a Hong Kong businessman, felt this practice was ineffective marketing:

> You have to hide [these promotions] and it leaks out. Hong Kong Disneyland has a $250 ticket and an $88 ticket, which includes a ticket for any resident of Hangzhou, but they can only go to Disneyland! You can only go to Disneyland for $88, and for Disney it is a gimmick to boost [attendance] numbers. This type of marketing is like when you take a tour and the tour guide takes you only to the jewelry shop where the tour guide gets a kickback. We are in the twenty-first century; grow up! . . . It cheapens the brand. (interview 2010)

Competition is another complicating factor. HKDL was mass-marketed through the Hong Kong media to the island's residents as a wondrous place that would make Hong Kong family-friendly and secure its status as a globally competitive city. For that reason, the expectations of Hong Kong residents were initially quite high. However, when these locals visited a Disneyland that turned out to be only 10 percent the size of Disney World in Florida, they were not impressed. For example, one of my interviewees who went during the opening days observed that HKDL was no bigger than Victoria Park, an average-sized urban park in Hong Kong. These savvy Hong Kong residents, many of whom had been to EPCOT and Disneyland in California, knew instantly that their Disneyland was microscopic in comparison and that it lacked the diverse attractions and thrill rides of other Disneyland parks: "[HKDL] is too small and expensive. They do not even have the Pirates of the Caribbean ride. People who have been to other Disneylands know it is not as good" (interview with local Disney enthusiast 2010). Realizing they were getting only 10 percent of a "true" Disney theme park, visitors felt cheated. Many of my informants reflected the same sentiment: the park was just too small. When I took my family to the park, they also complained that the park did not have enough attractions to occupy them for the whole day.

HKDL's marketing missteps might loom larger now that Hong Kong has lost its monopoly on the Disneyland experience in China. The new Shanghai Disneyland is five times larger than HKDL and easier for mainland Chinese visitors to access. The ongoing marketing of the new Shanghai Disneyland angered many of my Hong Kong informants, who regarded the new park as a threat to the viability of HKDL.

Some Hong Kong residents felt frustrated about the opening of Shanghai Disneyland, which will certainly have a negative impact on the Hong Kong Disneyland branch. As a tour guide in the mainland Chinese city of Guilin told me, "Chinese people are cost-conscious and given the choice to go to Hong Kong which is much more expensive or traveling in China—they will stay in China" (interview 2009). The implication is that Shanghai Disneyland could siphon off some of the mainland Chinese tourists from HKDL, and the effects could be disastrous when considering that these tourists represent nearly a third of all visitors to HKDL.

HKDL is often compared not only with other Disney theme parks in Asia and beyond but also with Japanese (kawaii) and Korean (hallyu) popular culture. One challenge faced by Disney in Asia is the popularity of other non-American popular cultures. For example, Korean all-girl bands such as Black Pink, Twice, and Red Velvet are famous all over Asia, including in Hong Kong. Top all-boy K-pop groups include BTS, EXO, and Wanna One. K-pop dance is also popular all over the world (Oh 2022).

Japanese popular culture is also ubiquitous throughout Hong Kong. On any given day on the subway an observer encounters countless young children and even young adults holding Japanese electronic toys, such as the Nintendo DSi and Sony PSP. Elaborate kawaii fashions and robot comics from Japan are also popular in Hong Kong. In *Millennial Monsters* (2006), Anne Allison describes how Pokémon, Sailor Moon, and the Power Rangers swept America and influenced a whole generation of young Americans. Allison argues that kawaii is popular because the characters are cute and flexible and cross the human-animal divide. I would add that Japanese popular culture has also influenced Asia and the rest of the globe. Many of my interviewees stated that Japanese and Korean popular cultures were more successful than American popular culture, a popularity that has likely had an impact on theme park attendance. One of the reasons for this greater success is a preference for Japanese stories because they are more open-ended and nuanced. As one of my informants explained, "Japan has its own animation. I talk with my friends about it. The Disney stories are very simple: good guys and bad guys; then they get married and it is over. That is very formulaic; the stuff we grew up with was much more complex. You cannot tell good from bad. The ending is ambiguous . . . sometimes it is not resolved, good or bad in your head. You have to work it out for yourself. In Disney stories, it is very clear what happened. Japanese animation is not like that" (interview, Hong Kong advertising executive, 2010).

Most of my Hong Kong interviewees preferred Japanese or Korean animation to Disney's animation. Anime-style shows, such as *Code Geass*, *Deathnotes*, *Bleach*, *Naruto*, and *Cowboy Bebop*, are wildly successful. These shows are different from traditional Disney animation in important ways, having greater complexity and involving deeper themes, such as colonialism. Furthermore, Japanese and Korean products and performances tend to cater to certain Asian aesthetic preferences; for example, the performers tend to be slender and light-skinned. One could also argue that these Korean and Japanese cultural products tap into underlying Confucian and Buddhist cultural principles that are shared among East Asian countries.

Another competitor of HKDL is the neighboring island of Macau, a former Portuguese colony that is famous for its casinos. Not everyone is looking to visit family-oriented places like theme parks; those who want a more adult experience without seeing any children might prefer Macau as a destination. Others might prefer real nature and real animals, and for them Ocean Park is a desirable destination. And as the next chapter will discuss, Ocean Park, also called the Hong Kong people's park, is a successful rival theme park in Hong Kong.

Conclusion

The people of Hong Kong have embraced American-style fast food and by doing so they might appear to be in the vanguard of a worldwide culinary revolution. But they have not been stripped of their cultural traditions, nor have they become "Americanized" in any but the most superficial of ways. Hong Kong people have been exposed to American brands, such as Starbucks, 7-Eleven, and KFC, that have undergone sinicization to appeal to Chinese or East Asian norms and tastes. McDonald's is an example of an American company that has adapted to Hong Kongers instead of the reverse. As mentioned earlier, it was McDonald's that trained people in Hong Kong to queue. When it first opened McDonald's had queuing issues because Hong Kongers of the time followed the Chinese norm of not standing in line. Accordingly, McDonald's hired line attendants to train its customers. McDonald's also offered a tailored menu, with items such as the mixed veggie egg mini twisty pasta Happy Meal, macaroni and ham pasta soups for breakfast, and sundaes in popular Asian flavors. Hong Kong locals appreciated the clean bathrooms at McDonald's and liked that it provided a rare space to sit all day in air-conditioned comfort, an appealing feature in Hong Kong given the very high humidity. Especially popular were the free napkins, breakfast items, and children's toys (Watson 1997). Unlike McDonald's in the United States, the restaurants in Hong Kong are typically safe, clean, and located in nice areas. Hong Kong McDonald's somehow became separated from America and turned into a "local" institution for an entire generation of affluent and middle-class consumers in Hong Kong (Watson 1997). Many people have positive memories of McDonald's in Hong Kong, and the younger generations who have grown up on the franchise feel it belongs to them. Some Hong Kong couples even get married at McDonald's; the phenomenon of "McWeddings" indicates how much McDonald's means to some Hong Kong locals.

Given the familiarity of American brands and fast food in Hong Kong, as exemplified by the success of McDonald's, HKDL should have been a runaway success. However, the attempts to indigenize the park to meet Hong Kongers' consumption needs ultimately failed. HKDL has not established itself as culturally appealing to locals. In the past, mainland Chinese often traveled to Hong Kong to get some western-consumption luxury items that they could not obtain in China.

Some of these name branded items are now becoming readily available in mainland China. This would make Hong Kong lose these mainland Chinese customers, although wealthy Asians from South Asia and Southeast Asia may still travel to Hong Kong for western goods. One of my informants contended that mainland Chinese tourists gained prestige and the admiration of others by going to HKDL (oral history, local Hong Kong mother, 2012). In contrast, the Hong Kong residents I interviewed referred to their social status and sophistication to explain their conscious decision *not* to visit HKDL. This helped to distinguish them on the grounds of cultural capital from the mainland Chinese tourists who visited. Whether the park is considered a success or a failure, however, Disney will continue to receive royalties from Hong Kong Disneyland.

2
Labor Indigenization
Cultural Imperialist Attitudes

> Disney asked for a lot of things and used the [Hong Kong] taxpayers' money to pay for them. Disney made Hong Kong pay for the entire infrastructure. Disney wanted specific trees throughout the park. They had to come from the United States or Southeast Asia, along with the soil mix they needed, which was very expensive! The taxes of Hong Kong people paid for all of that. Even though we all worked together, [American] Disney workers gave the impression that they are superior to us [Hong Kong Disney workers]. (interview, Emily Liu, HKDL engineer, 2012)

On a hot and humid July day in 2012, I met Emily at a coffeehouse in Hong Kong.[1] Emily was a thirty-two-year-old engineer who was working on the structural development of Hong Kong Disneyland. As we spoke, Emily expressed her discontentment about the unequal treatment she was receiving as one of over seven thousand laborers who were involved in the park's construction. Although she referred to the Disneyland project as "a Rolls Royce construction"—a good

DRAWING 3. HKDL gate. (Credit: Sally Pirie.)

construction project physically—she went on to add, "Maybe we needed just a Honda Civic construction and the cost was too high" (interview 2012).

Emily's opinion that HKDL was a physically well-built structure was not uncommon among the workers I interviewed at the park. Like many other workers, however, she did not have a positive view of the way she and other HKDL workers were treated: she said she was treated poorly in comparison to the American engineers. Other workers made similar comments and added that they cared little for the indigenization attempts of the HKDL developers. By this, they meant that they were unimpressed with the developers' attempts to be accommodating to the local culture.[2]

This chapter examines the workers' view of HKDL to evaluate whether the transnational theme park successfully accommodated the needs and interests of the local community in relation to labor. Based on an examination of labor records from HKDL and interviews with workers involved in constructing and running the park, I argue that HKDL's indigenization has been incomplete on the labor front due to the original unequal contract between the Hong Kong SAR and the Walt Disney Company, bad publicity, and ongoing labor disputes. Although HKDL was promoted to the public as a high-quality employment opportunity for indigenous Hong Kong residents, the well-paying positions available to Hong Kong locals once the park was complete turned out to be far fewer than promised, and those who were hired describe ongoing inequalities in their labor conditions based on nationality and ethnic group. Notably, my interviewees expressed that U.S. Disney workers projected an attitude of superiority and treated them unfairly. Despite Disney's indigenization attempts, my interviewees reported they did not love the Disney ethos; at best they thought of Disneyland as just another place to work, and at worst they criticized it as an abusive workplace. The Main Street USA simulacrum located in Hong Kong may seem at first glance to embody the idyllic Walt Disney dream, but—according to interviews with workers and my own observations—it is rife with employment inequality.

The HKDL project was promoted by the political and business elite as a panacea for the high unemployment rates in Hong Kong in the eighties and nineties. As noted above, the Hong Kong government said that the park would provide thousands of high-quality jobs for indigenous Hong Kong workers. Mittermeier (2021, 159) says one of the biggest issues Hong Kong Disneyland faced is labor. One has to unpack what the indigenous labor force thinks about their employment and who can be considered a local Hong Kong worker. The word "indigenous" apparently did not apply at the executive level, as the majority of the top executives of HKDL turned out to be of Anglo-American descent. Disney's ability to employ an international, intranational, and transnational labor force complicated the hiring of a true indigenized labor force in Hong Kong. It is no surprise, then, that Disney's attempt to adapt to a local workforce had a rocky beginning.

Labor Indigenization: Just Another Job

HKDL's workers have rarely been asked whether Disney's attempts to accommodate the local community have been successful. In this section, I highlight the sentiments of HKDL workers who reflected on whether or not the indigenization of the park was effective for them. The employees included a middle manager (Mr. Lam), an engineer (Mr. Liu), a dancer (Mr. Reyes), and an executive manager (Mr. Smith) (see table 1). The first two were Hong Kong locals, the third was Filipino, and the fourth was British. My interviewees described labor indigenization at Disney as problematic and in flux, citing the unequal treatment of workers of different ethnicities as a reason.

TABLE 1. List of interviewees

PSEUDONYM	GENDER	HKDL POSITION	NATIONALITY	AGE
Reyes	Male	Dancer	Filipino	28
Lam	Male	Middle manager	Hong Kong	47
Liu	Female	Engineer	Hong Kong	32
Smith	Male	Executive	British	57

SOURCES: Semiformal interviews with the author, 2010–2014.

Ms. Liu was thirty-two years old and had been one of the many American and Hong Kong engineers involved in the park's construction. She had learned about Disney as a child and had visited all of the world's Disney parks. As she witnessed the many stages of the park's development, she concluded that the American engineers looked down on the Hong Kong engineers. Ms. Liu did not believe HKDL had fair labor practices. Ms. Liu said she was aware, for example, that the costumed workers did not get adequate breaks and were not treated well. She also mentioned the environmental controversies over the building of the park. When I asked about her feelings about Disney and her employment with Disney, she said that Disney had a lot of "wants": the corporation wanted Hong Kong to create the infrastructure exactly as Disney designed and planned. The landscape design was performed entirely by Disney. Without input from Hong Kong residents, the Hong Kong government selected the environmentally controversial Penny Bay for the site of the park and gave it to Disney free of charge. Ms. Liu stated that building the park was a huge job with a tight time frame. The job was made more difficult because Penny Bay had no roads or infrastructure. It was also controversial because many fish were killed in the process. "I won't give any more money to Disneyland," said Ms. Liu. On the several occasions that her job had taken her to HKDL, she refused to eat anything while she was there. She was very disappointed in the HKDL Halloween party and noted that Ocean Park's and Tokyo Disney's Halloween events were much better in execution. She was adamant that the Hong Kong taxpayers had already given enough to Disney. I asked her why she felt taxpayers had been duped: "The partnership is not even!" she exclaimed.

Mr. Lam told me that people of all ages worked for HKDL. Some worked there because it was Disney and they were attracted by the company's Western/U.S. branding. For him, however, working at HKDL was simply an opportunity for advancement: "The offer was good and not the same as my other Hong Kong jobs." He said that Disney's work culture was quite different from the work culture in Hong Kong. Disney has multiple guidelines and a strong commitment to its culture. Although he stated that Disney had a different work culture than his previous jobs, he had no opinion on whether it was better or worse. Most HKDL workers saw it just as another job, in contrast to U.S. Disney workers, who often describe themselves as Disneyphiles.

Mr. Lam maintained that the majority of the workers were Chinese from Hong Kong and very few were American employees. The Filipino and mainland Chinese dancers and singers were the main exception: "Filipino workers are employed in the area of entertainment, they can dance and sing better than locals," said Mr. Lam.[3] In the future, he believed, there would be a tendency to hire more workers from mainland China because they would work for lower wages than Hong Kong residents. Because the mainland workers could cross the border to go home, it was unnecessary to provide them with housing. Filipino workers were more expensive to hire because they were paid more than mainland Chinese workers and had to fly to Hong Kong from the Philippines. Mr. Lam also communicated some of the negative aspects of working at Disney, specifically what he called a superiority complex exhibited by some of the Anglo-American managers. He also stated that he knew of some workers who felt they were treated unfairly by management.

Mr. Reyes, who was twenty-eight years old, had not become interested in Disney cartoons until he was eleven years old. In his early twenties, he applied to HKDL because he wanted to perform. He knew many types of dance, including hip-hop, ballet, and jazz. His two-day audition and interview with Disney took place at the Music School of Ryan Cayabyab in the Philippines, where he was told to "help bring the magic to life!" The minimum age requirement for dance auditions was eighteen years. Disney representatives taught the performers a routine to be used in the audition. Mr. Reyes's audition took two hours, during which time he was asked to perform several routines. Over a two-day period, two hundred to four hundred people tried out, and perhaps fifty to two hundred were hired for each show. The ethnic composition of the Hong Kong Disney labor force, he reported, was primarily Chinese, Filipino, and American. After a successful audition, Reyes danced in the "Lion King" and "Golden Mickey" shows at HKDL. Although he loved performing, he was aware that the workers were not treated equally. Americans received a housing allowance and sometimes free housing, which the Filipinos did not receive. He felt that the management was not fair, admitting freely that he "disliked the system—there is some discrimination in treatment. It is not fair! There is more attention [given] to the Chinese. For example, Filipino dancers [must give] more 'runs' [performances] than Chinese dancers. Filipinos sometimes have to dance four or five runs when the Chinese [dance] only two runs." Mr. Reyes went on to say that he did not care for Disney's indigenization attempts in spatial arrangements, language, and food.

Mr. Smith, aged fifty-seven years, was an HKDL executive who had been a fan of Disney since he was a child. When asked what he thought of the indigenization of space, labor, and consumption, he seemed positive but vague. He mentioned that he thought that Hong Kong and Asian people in general had a very strong work ethic: "Their work ethic is better than Western workers. Westerners will never work as hard as these Asian workers." He commented that when HKDL first opened it sold "garish sequined HKDL tops" because that is what the mainland Chinese preferred, but over the years he had observed that the mainland Chinese were dressing more in line with the global norms. The park still sells HKDL sequined tops and hats, but not as many as it did at first. He said that he had heard complaints of unequal treatment and salary disputes by the workers. Mr. Smith thought the food was fine and the three languages that the park catered to were a good effort at indigenization for local and international visitors. Smith was especially complimentary toward the two HKDL hotels, noting that they were staffed well and run efficiently and had been designed with the principles of feng shui in mind.

All of these interviewees either felt or had heard that HKDL workers were not being treated equally. Three of the four reported that in their experience, Anglo-American Disney employees looked down on employees of other nationalities and/or imposed harsher working conditions on them. Even the interviewees who had not received unfair treatment themselves had heard the reports that workers were being subjected to unpleasant and often unequal labor practices. These interviews suggest that HKDL has not met the needs of the Hong Kong workforce. Although the park has provided some jobs, it has not provided an indigenized workplace. And as the next section will show, these four interviewees' comments are far from an aberration; on the contrary, they are indicative of a broader pattern in Hong Kong workers' and residents' perceptions of HKDL.

Labor-Related Criticisms of HKDL

Complaints about labor violations preceded the official 2005 opening of the park. Disney could not control the major initial negative publicity about labor improprieties that the construction workers brought to light. The builders of the park, including some Hong Kong indigenous local workers, complained that Disney did not pay them for some of their work, which resulted in a protest outside the Disney gates. It should be noted that the construction workers were not hired by Disney: in a process that is relatively common among multinational corporations, HKDL outsourced the construction work to contract companies, which then hired the workers. HKDL paid the subcontracted company, but the money was not passed on to the workers.

Many Hong Kong residents, including all of my interviewees, became aware of these labor violations because they heard and saw a constant barrage of negative publicity. The complaints of workers before HKDL opened further complicated the reports of labor difficulties after the opening of the park. HKDL did not respond swiftly to the labor abuse allegations, although they were very widely reported. (In general, Disney is secretive about its practices.) Like Disney, the Hong Kong government was not forthcoming in its response to local construction worker claims. The ongoing labor protests primed Hong Kong residents to be wary of the promises of the HKDL project (ReviewTyme 2018).

Hong Kong labor laws are not especially powerful because the government tries to be "noninterventionist," which implies that the workers at HKDL lack a strong legal footing for their complaints due to a lack of governmental support. Disney already had a long history of being antiunion and antilabor in its U.S. theme parks and housing developments. For example, although Disneyland has its own official Disney human resources group where workers can report complaints, workers often do not feel comfortable complaining to an internal human resources organization. HKDL does have an independent union called the Hong Kong

Disneyland Cast Members Union; in 2006, this union reported many new staff complaints, including low pay, ill treatment, and injuries. In 2016, HKDL staff held sit-ins to protest the mass layoffs.

Labor is a sensitive issue in Hong Kong. As described in the introduction, from the fifties through the eighties, Hong Kong was considered one of the world's sweatshops, producing everything from plastic flowers to transistor radios (Chiu and Lee 1997). Much of this labor was performed by young women who sacrificed their vitality working in the factories, helping to make Hong Kong the economic "tiger" it is now. After 1978, when China opened its so-called bamboo curtain to the West, many Hong Kong factories began to transfer to Guangdong in what was one of the most rapid cases of deindustrialization in world history. By the 1980s, millions of the Hong Kong residents—especially women—who had worked in these sweatshops were middle-aged, jobless, and facing age-related employment discrimination. These factory workers, who were not formally educated, felt abandoned; with no further prospect of high-paying work (Chiu and Lee 1997), some retreated back to their homes or were forced to settle for jobs with much lower salaries. The government, instead of committing resources to reeducating them, invested in HKDL in an effort to increase the number of local jobs. The park, in short, was touted as a potential economic savior at a time when Hong Kong was facing rising unemployment and the flight of labor and capital in the wake of deindustrialization and in anticipation of the handover of Hong Kong to China. HKDL was predicted to generate profits of US$19 billion in forty years and to bring in more than 5.6 million visitors.

Neither of these predictions came to fruition, although a number of jobs were created: "Disney and other companies, they say, will create an estimated 18,000 new jobs by the time the park opens. And total job creation will grow to 36,000 when Hong Kong Disneyland reaches full build-out" (Lyne 2004). Moreover, as discussed in chapter 1, the HKDL deal was widely perceived as unfair to the Hong Kong government and by extension to Hong Kong's taxpayers. Activist organizations, such as Students and Scholars Against Corporate Misbehaviour (SACOM) and anonymous anti-Disney activists who call themselves "Disney Hunters," protested the unfair HKDL deal. They asserted that the money should have been used to help Hong Kong's indigent citizens:

> I think it was the financial crisis in 1997. It was not something from the people, the ordinary people. [The government needs to] generate more work opportunities. . . . In 1997 many Hong Kong people desperately wanted to improve the economic situation. We must have a lot of land restoration. It was an unfair agreement with the Hong Kong government. The Hong Kong government must invest a lot of money, but we do not have a lot of sovereignty. We think the agreement is unfair. Disney has no transparency about what they earn . . . in these processes Hong Kong citizens cannot voice their concern. (Disney hunter interviewee 2016)

In the midst of a housing affordability crisis in Hong Kong, these critics believed, the government could have put the money spent on HKDL into affordable housing projects. In addition, some Hong Kong labor leaders thought of Disney as a culturally imperialistic neocolonizer. "They are trying to make Hong Kong a colony of Disney," complained labor leader and legislator Lee Cheuk-yan (Wiseman 2005). In what might be described as an expression of contemporary Orientalism (see Said 1978), the Hong Kong colonial government chose to invest money in a Western behemoth rather than a local venture, as if Hong Kong lacked the confidence to develop its own cultural products. Edward Said defines Orientalism as "a western style of dominating, restructuring, and having authority over the Orient" (1978, 3). It must be noted, however, that Hong Kong is a unique space in relation to neocolonialism: just as Disney is accused of neocolonialism in Hong Kong, many of its residents accuse mainland China of the same.

Asian American activists created a storm on X (formerly called Twitter) over the live-action film *Mulan* (2020). They accuse the writers of the original screenplay to have written a film with a white savior plot (Banh 2020a). There was additional controversy in Hong Kong when the main actress of *Mulan* said she supported the Hong Kong police. The Hong Kong prodemocracy protestors have called for a boycott of the live-action *Mulan* (2020) film. In the film credits, there was a "special thanks" to the Xinjiang authorities, which some believed bowed to the Chinese government. Academics said that Disney was self-censoring to appease the Chinese market. Hong Kong activists contend this ignores the alleged ethnic, linguistic, religious, and labor suppressions in Xinjiang. Disney also did not allow an episode of the adult animation cartoon *Simpsons* on "forced child labor camps" to play in Hong Kong.[4] There has been a back-and-forth kaleidoscope of labor inequality complaints from multiple parties.

It is worth pointing out that in addition to eliciting labor complaints, HKDL has failed to make a net profit in most of the years of its operation. The total net profit or loss figures for the years of 2006 and 2007 when it first opened were not released, to the ire of the Hong Kong residents who had paid for the majority of the park. Nonetheless, it was reported that the first two years were unprofitable. In 2008, there was a loss of over US$200 million, followed by a 2009 loss of over

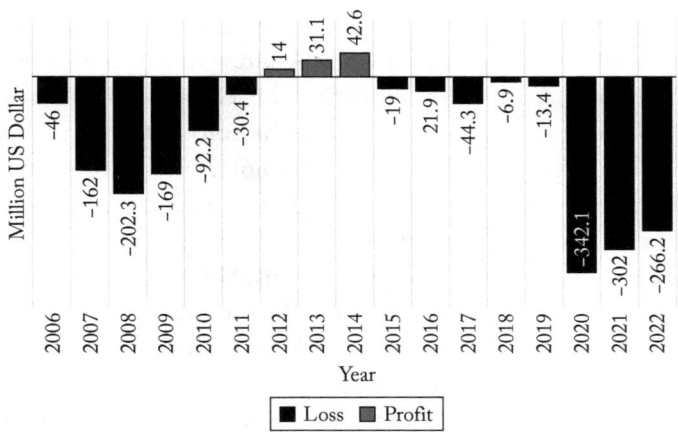

FIGURE 8. Hong Kong Disneyland annual profit/loss 2006–2022. (Credit: Sanjay Soundarajan.)

US$160 million (see figure 8). The losses continued until 2011, and from 2012 to 2014 net profits were in the range of US$10–40 million. From 2015 onward, the park has recorded a net loss. Other than the three years of 2012 to 2014 there has been a significant loss each year, especially during the COVID-19 pandemic. After the pandemic closings there were intermittent openings and closings. Hong Kong itself closed its borders and then had one of the most stringent quarantine policies where international travelers had to sequester for thirty days or more until they were permitted to enter freely in Hong Kong. As of 2024 the park still does not open every day, and this surely affects the profit margins.

Hong Kong Profit

Since HKDL was conceived, it has had a revolving door of managing directors. Steven Tight was the managing director at the inception of HKDL in 2001. The position was passed in turn to long-term Disney executives Don

Robinson (2001–2005) and William Ernest (2006–2008). The next managing director was Andrew Kam (2008–2016), a former Coca-Cola executive in China who turned HKDL into a profitable venture in 2010 but resigned in 2016 for "personal reasons" (Sun 2016). His departure was stunning enough, but his next step sent shockwaves through the tourism community: he was hired by and has since become president of Disney's chief rival in mainland China, Wanda Themed Entertainment. The founder of the Dailan Wanda Group, Wang Jianlin, who is China's richest man, has publicly stated that he will "squash" Shanghai Disneyland and make it nonprofitable within ten or twenty years (Cendrowski 2016). In an interview reported in *Fortune*, he warns, "They [Disney] shouldn't have entered China. We have a [saying]: one tiger is no match for a pack of wolves. Shanghai has one Disney, while Wanda, across the nation, will open 15 to 20." Succeeding Kam as managing director of HKDL was Samuel Lau, a Hong Kong native who started with Disney in 2010. Stephanie Young took over the leadership in 2018 before leaving in 2020 to become president of consumer products, games, and publishing for Disney. In 2020, Michael Moriarty, a fourteen-year Disney veteran, was named the new managing director and chief financial officer for HKDL.

With seven people holding the position of managing director at HKDL from 2005 to 2025, there has been no long-term continuity in executive leadership. Leadership succession is Inevitable, but excessive, turnover can be disruptive for employees as it affects morale, and the direction of the organization can change with each new director. Furthermore, incoming directors often lack historical knowledge of the organization. Leaders who do not have institutional familiarity with the HDKL corporation can be unprepared when catastrophes like the COVID-19 pandemic hit. Such managing director turnover has left HKDL ill-equipped to deal with the allegations of labor abuse.

Ongoing Labor Issues

A number of HKDL's labor problems stem from Disney policies intended to maintain the "magical" illusion that its spaces are separated from the real world. One such regulation states that the identities of police and other public agency workers must be concealed. Accordingly, when Hong Kong Disneyland opened to the public on September 12, 2005, health inspectors were forced to remove their badges when they came into the park because of worries that they would alarm the guests. This was an unprecedented affront to Hong Kong governmental agency workers and would not have been tolerated in other parts of Hong Kong. Disney also has a comprehensive grooming and dress policy. For example, standard Disney regulations for employees insist on no beards, colored hair, long hair, or cell phone use. Costumed Disney employees are given a standard period of time for rest; however, Hong Kong Disneyland employees were not given the same amount of time as Disney's costumed employees in Florida and California: they were "given only 15 minutes rest time every four hours, whereas their US counterparts rest after two" (Dembina 2005). The weather in Hong Kong can be extremely hot and humid, and Disneyland workers get very hot in their costumes. Labor activists have charged Disney with forcing staff to work eleven- and thirteen-hour days, providing inadequate breaks, and rewriting daily work schedules without notice. Many of the Hong Kong locals I interviewed stated that they were aware of these infractions because they had been well publicized. Local community

TABLE 2. HKDL labor grievances

Superior attitude of Disney
Builders of HKDL underpaid
Food and health inspectors forced to remove badges
Hot costumed characters and less break time
Unequal pay between workers
Overwork: Forcing staff to work 11- and 13-hour days
Rewriting daily work schedules without notice
Dozens of employees leaving jobs

SOURCES: SACOM (2013); Choi (2012); and Banh (2019b)

members have also expressed dismay at the amount of bad publicity the park has received in the media. There were reports of employees have left their jobs because they felt they were mistreated and not being properly promoted (Choi 2012). The original marketing team was given word that they were dismissed in the morning and had to clear out by the afternoon (interview, HKDL marketer, 2010).

Another labor problem arises from Disney's requirement for performative labor. This type of labor had proven difficult for both staff and visitors in France, and it was similarly hard to implement in Hong Kong, as "in Hong Kong, people who are overly friendly are looked upon with suspicion" (Matusitz 2011, 675). HKDL workers also report that when they "make eye contact and smile at local customers, customers may feel suspicious of the smile and some even intimidated [sic] and reply, 'What are you laughing at?' others may feel nervous and go away" (Choi 2007, 325). Disruptive behavior by many guests, such as frequent quarrels or outright fights, queue jumping, and even public urination, exacerbates the employees' difficulties (Choi 2012, 391). When the park began to struggle with lower-than-expected attendance, the situation became even worse for staff as cost-cutting measures were put in place. Consequently, early reviews of the park were not positive (Mittermeier 2021).

Conclusion

In his policy speeches from 1997 to 2000, then–Hong Kong chief executive Tung Chee-Hwa promoted HKDL to the Hong Kong people as an opportunity for the employment of indigenous or local labor (SACOM 2013). As discussed in chapter 1, several factors laid the groundwork for the Disney–Hong Kong partnership, such as the 1997 return to China, the avian flu outbreak, and the Asian financial crisis, all of which took a negative toll on the workers of Hong Kong by severely reducing job opportunities. Later, the 2003 SARS outbreak and the terrorist attacks on September 11, 2001, further reduced international travel to Hong Kong. It was hoped that the gap left by these events, as well as the economic void created by the departure of many industries, would be filled by HKDL. As hoped, the theme park has provided some much-needed jobs for Hong Kong residents, although not as many as projected. Whether the park has provided an indigenized workplace, however, is much less certain. Labor violation claims were filed even before the park opened, and a steady stream of mainland Chinese sweatshop labor injustice claims have been publicized (SACOM 2013).

In my interviews, some HKDL workers expressed they were treated unequally because of their nationality and ethnicity, perhaps because of an attitude of cultural imperialism on the part of members of other nationalities. The Hong Kong engineer I interviewed believed that the American engineers felt superior to their Hong Kong counterparts. The middle manager acknowledged that he was treated well but said he knew of both happy and unhappy employee situations. The Filipino dancers I spoke with complained that they were forced to dance more shows than dancers of other nationalities, such as Americans and Hong Kong locals. The

HKDL executive was the most positive about the indigenization attempts in the domains of food and space, but he had heard that there were labor complaints. HKDL workers showed resistance to unfair treatment by refusing to engage in certain forms of emotional labor, such as constantly smiling and saying "Have a magical day" to every guest; by refusing to financially support the theme park; and sometimes by quitting their jobs.

Full indigenization may not work in a place like Hong Kong, or by extension in HKDL, because so much of its identity is formed by the transience of people from other countries. One has to constantly interrogate what is indigenous labor in Hong Kong with no many transnational migrants who settle for a while in Hong Kong and then leave. There is the other group of former Hong Kong citizens who return with another passport. These groups have varying degrees of identity, with some who staunchly say that Hong Kong identity is something unique and is not connected to mainland China. By contrast, you have individuals who have Hong Kong citizenship who support mainland Chinese identity and everything in between. Then there are variations of identity based on Chinese regional identity and migration year to Hong Kong. There is a situational pragmatism that many Hong Kongers have about their identity. HKDL labor indigenization is further complicated by the inclusion of an international, intranational, and transnational HKDL workforce.

3

Spatial Indigenization

Creating a Heterotopia

Today is a typically hot and humid day in Hong Kong. After a long wait, my family and I finally enter the Metro Transit Railway (MTR) line train that connects to Hong Kong Disneyland (HKDL: 香港迪士尼公園). For 30 minutes, we are crammed like human sardines into the hard metal train on the Tung Chung 東涌綫 line, before we quickly transfer trains to the navy-hued and luxurious Disneyland Resort Line 迪士尼綫 train. Controversially, this line is fully paid for by the city-state of Hong Kong, even though it goes only to Disneyland. When we enter the Disneyland Resort Line train, half the people are gone, and it suddenly feels as though we are alone, an experience that is unheard of at most Disneylands.

On the Disneyland Resort Line train, we are transported to a Victorian-themed architectural space of metal and rich dark fabrics. I gaze at the walls of this specially made train, covered with velvety materials, and notice the seats with soft, plush cushions; a large sculpture of Mickey Mouse garbed as a wizard is in a glass case with stars scattered everywhere. The Mickey Mouse in the case brings to mind Mickey's appearance in the Sorcerer's Apprentice segment of Fantasia. *Soon the train stops and we get off.*

> *My family and I realize that we still need to climb a steep flight of stairs or take an escalator to reach the park level. This is a deliberate Disneyesque design feature. A Disney engineer told me that Walt Disney wanted a space that guests could not look out of and bystanders could not look into. One element that Disney engineers always include in a space is an isolated fort-like enclosure in which they can control all of the spatial elements. Entering a Disney space is supposed to feel fantastical, but I feel sad about how much this space cost the Hong Kong people. It is widely advertised as a culturally sensitive space with many feng shui 風水 elements. The public relations material promised that HKDL would be respectful of Hong Kong's people and culture, but instead it is essentially a carbon copy of the original California Disneyland with some strange Orientalized features. I see nothing of Hong Kong here.*

Around the time HKDL opened, a number of news articles that read like public relations marketing pieces appeared in the press claiming that the park was culturally competent and sensitive to Hong Kong's people and culture. An article by Laura Holson titled "The Feng Shui Kingdom" (2005b) stated, "Heeding the advice of a feng shui consultant is one of many steps Disney executives have taken at the park to reflect the local culture—and to make sure they do not repeat some mistakes of the past." Among these mistakes were controversies surrounding Disneyland Paris (formerly Euro Disneyland), in which Disney was accused of cultural imperialism and of committing the faux pas of not serving wine. Numerous articles on HKDL that appeared at this time reported that the Walt Disney Company was honoring local customs and culture by using feng shui spatial practices.

Disney's press releases gave the impression that the company was sincerely listening to the wants and needs of Hong Kong locals and responding in a sensitive manner. Disney

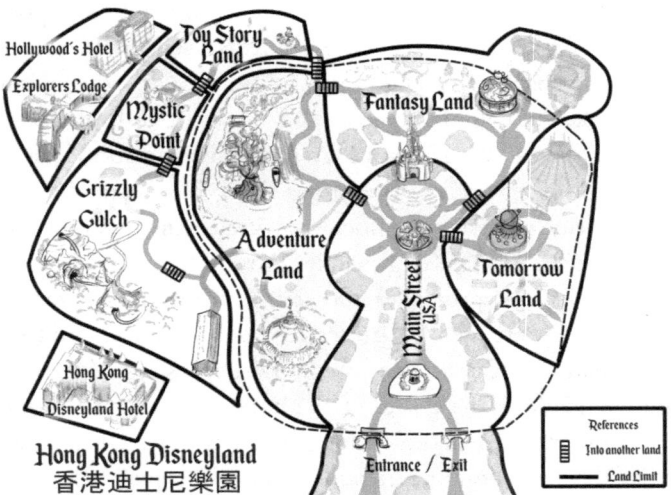

MAP 1. Hong Kong Disneyland. (Credit: Viviana Moyano.)

has faced multiple accusations of being insensitive in its depictions of race, culture, and gender (Banh 2020a and 2020b), and Disney cartoons, such as those featuring Donald Duck, have been used to promote capitalist ideology in Chile (Dorfman and Mattelart 1975). In the lead-up to the opening of Hong Kong Disneyland, consequently, Disney was keen to promote an impression of cultural sensitivity by advertising its use of the Chinese art of feng shui. Feng shui (traditional Chinese: 風水; simplified Chinese: 风水; pinyin: fēng shuǐ; literally, "wind-water") is an ancient Chinese scientific practice or art that uses the laws of heaven (astronomy) and earth (geography) to direct the flow of the circulating life energy *chi* (気, qi). As a design concept, feng shui is supposed to bring synchronization and serenity to a space.

In this chapter, I describe the HKDL space as a heterotopia with layers of meaning that link back to colonial violence. Through the use of feng shui practices and

Spatial Indigenization 75

"Asian"-inspired architecture, Disney has attempted to portray the park as a utopian space of cultural sensitivity. However, the space of HKDL can also be seen as a dystopian palimpsest of colonial violence, having been built on unexploded World War II bombs (Associated Press 2001). There are also spaces such as the Hong Kong Hotel and Mystic Manor ride that show an idealized Victorian time that did not exist for Hong Kong people. I argue that the attempts to use feng shui principles and architectural indigenization at the park were merely Orientalized performances and that few visitors notice or care about Disney's so-called space indigenization. The spaces of the hotels are very well made with exceptional natural Hong Kong waters. Ultimately, HKDL can be best understood as a budget copy of the original Anaheim Disneyland, with fewer themed spaces or rides than other Disneylands, likely because of Disney's financial problems with Disneyland Paris. Meanwhile, there is no dedicated space in HKDL that depicts Hong Kong's culture, history, or people.

Hong Kong Disneyland as Heterotopia and Utopia

As one of the largest and most powerful multimedia corporations in the world, the Walt Disney Company is fully capable of transforming large spaces. The company owns live-action productions, animated productions, studios, theme parks, television stations, and radio stations and accrues millions of dollars in revenue every year. Disney even operates whole towns designed to its specifications, such as Celebration, Florida (Ross 2000). Disney's theme parks contribute to local economies worldwide and bring in tourism money. Disney is also very savvy in making deals: as discussed in the preceding chapter, for example, Hong Kong paid 90 percent of the costs of the park but currently has only

57 percent ownership while Disney has 43 percent ownership. The Hong Kong SAR and Hong Kong people were encouraged to accept this deal because of the "competition-development" discourse and "disappearing-world-city" discourse in various media. "Hong Kong had detractors of the HKDL project. An elected legislator in the city argued that the HKDL deal was an "Unequal Treaty" because the HK SAR government had invested HK$22.95 billion compared with the Walt Disney Company's HK$2.45 billion" (Choi 2010a, 574).

Disney's space transformation process is intentionally invisible and generates the kind of mixed reality described by Michel Foucault as a "heterotopia," a term that signifies a place that has multiple meanings and relationships beyond what any given person sees. Different people experience the same thing differently, as if they exist in parallel dimensions. By calling such unconstrained "spaces within spaces" heterotopias, Foucault denies them the status of utopias but also distinguishes them from dystopias. Heterotopias, which can be violent and uncontrolled or the opposite, include prisons, motel rooms, and theme parks. A heterotopia, in Foucault's formulation, has two functions: the heterotopia of illusion creates a space of illusion in relation to all of the remaining spaces that exposes every real space, and the heterotopia of compensation creates a real space—a space that is other (Foucault 1986).

As a heterotopia, HKDL performs both of these functions. It is important to recognize, however, that like other Disneylands, HKDL presents itself as a utopia with its well-known public relations phrase the "happiest place on earth." The castles are built to denote European folktales, fantasy, and innocence. Main Street USA is supposed to evoke an idyllic midwestern town. HKDL Christmas is awash with holiday-related objects to buy. Large trash cans are hidden away from the public, who are called "guests." The staff are instructed to say "Have a magical day" when guests arrive and leave the park. Baudrillard famously called Disneyland "a perfect model of all entangled orders of simulacra. It is first a play on illusions and phantasms; The Pirates, The Frontier, the Future World etc." (1994, 12).

Attempting to build a utopian theme park in the real world, however, comes with an inherent contradiction: whereas a utopia is by definition a not-place, a theme park is located on a particular piece of land within a specific political jurisdiction, in a place with its own local and regional cultural norms. To build HKDL, then, Disney had to make the physical space of the park seem appealing to Hong Kong's people and to an extent also to the visitors from elsewhere in East Asia whom Disney hoped to attract—making it a sort of heterotopia, in the sense that the park juxtaposes "several sites that are in themselves incompatible" (Foucault 1986, 25). In other words, as I discuss throughout this book, Disney had to indigenize the park. Its success, as I show throughout this chapter, was limited.

SPATIAL INDIGENIZATION THROUGH FENG SHUI

One important way Disney sought to indigenize the space of the park was by applying the principles of feng shui. Feng shui, a Chinese invention, is a cosmological and geomancy-based system for placing structures that is thought to ensure good fortune and avoid disaster. Some aspects of feng shui involve trying to predict the future by examining the outer terrestrial environment, such as mountains and streams. It is claimed that by looking at the environment, a practitioner can divine energy flows and discover hidden knowledge. Feng shui likely originated from Taoism's questioning of the place of humans in the universe. By the end of the Han dynasty (206 B.C.E.–220 C.E.), feng shui was being used to establish an abstract order through practical engineering and agricultural projects. Feng shui became intermeshed with Buddhism during the Song dynasty (960–1279), which is known as the golden age of Buddhism in East Asia, and was used to determine how pagodas and temples were placed. This system was used in ancient China and later spread to Korea, Vietnam, and Japan. Its application was extended to numerology, auspicious dates and times, and even burials. Later it came to encompass many other architectural features. The principles of feng shui include everything from how a house should be built to how everything should be placed inside it, with attention to numbers, colors, shapes, and sounds. For Chinese businesses, feng shui is considered crucial for attracting customers and protecting the business from revenue loss. In many parts of Asia, feng shui is used in the hope it will bring luck, harmony, and wealth to households and businesses (Associated Press 2005).

In designing HKDL, Disney integrated the five elements of feng shui: wood, fire, earth, metal, and water. In practice, these elements must be used throughout an area in accordance with specific placement principles. A space that is not arranged in the proper configuration is thought to invite bad luck and ruin to a household or business. For Disney, using these elements was an easy choice: "'Many believe bad feng shui . . . can cause financial ruin, and Disney wasn't about to risk it,' said Tom Morris, a chief designer at Hong Kong Disneyland" (Hui 2005). Table 3 shows how the five elements are represented at HKDL, based on the park's media releases. To avoid fire hazards, fire is illustrated on television screens. Earth is represented by placing rocks throughout the park. Ponds and other water elements are scattered throughout the park, and metal appears in the form of gold figurines that are sold in the gift shop and an ancient-looking gold boat. The park has numerous wooden elements and abundant trees.

TABLE 3. Five elements of feng shui at HKDL

Fire: 消防	In the Mickey and Lion King show there is prominent fire.
Earth: 地球	There are rocks in front of the hotel and in the park and Inspiration Lake.
Water: 水	Water features are seen in the fountains and lakes.
Metal: 的金屬	Gold jewelry for Character are sold.
Wood: 木	Trees should be plentiful according to good feng shui ideals, and many have been planted both inside and outside the park.

All of these elements can be questioned. Does a fire on a screen count as fire for the purposes of feng shui? The boulders, according to Kirsten Day, do not seem to have been placed in any specific manner: "No boulders appeared to be unusually located, in line with a feng shui placement. There are a number of rocks and boulders that are part of the Adventureland theme, but there was nothing inconsistent with any of the other theme parks and the Disneyland stage setting of the area" (Day 2015, 261). As for water, metal, and wood, these are common at all Disneyland parks, so they do not seem to represent feng shui elements particular to HKDL. For example, there are many water features in other Disney parks (Day 2015, 262).

Disney also purportedly applied the principles of feng shui when designing the park's gate. When the train stops at the Disneyland station, a visitor faces the HKDL gate. HKDL claims that the park is situated on Lantau Island in Penny Bay because the island was considered "auspicious" and energy-producing by unnamed feng shui experts (Associated Press 2005). The green gate has red lettering that reads "Hong Kong Disneyland Resort" (香港迪士尼樂園). The Associated Press (2005) has reported that HKDL's gate was designed in line with a specific element of feng shui geomancy, tilted twelve degrees in a north/south direction to achieve maximum good fortune and prevent the luck from washing out to sea.

According to Day, however, the design of the main HKDL entrance likely had more to do with crowd control than with feng shui. The entrance that "runs along the north-south axis is the pedestrian walkway from the car parks and the Disney MTR station. Traditionally the most auspicious direction for entry is south facing. The actual entry to the theme park is located on an east-west axis" (Day 2015, 235–250). It appears that the gate is really a control mechanism, and moreover that Hong Kong locals are unlikely to see or gain anything from this feng shui element. It is doubtful whether any of the visitors or staff noticed or cared about these "indigenized" HKDL gate features that were so widely broadcast in the media. In the case of the HKDL gate, the supposed feng shui elements seem to represent a neoliberal multiculturalism that pays lip service to indigenization while masking a typical Disney crowd-control feature.

Consider Disney's use of another aspect of feng shui: color. The auspicious colors of feng shui are red, blue, green, and white. Red in particular is a lucky color in China, and it is no accident that the lettering on many of the gates, posters, and signs at HKDL is deep crimson. The dress of some of the Disney characters, including Minnie and Mickey Mouse, was changed in order to more closely reflect Cantonese culture: Mickey is shown wearing a traditional Mandarin red costume and Minnie is shown wearing a *qipao*, which is a ceremonial Chinese red and gold dress. Much of the merchandise sold at the park features a combination of several colors and shapes. The stores feature a range of very colorful merchandise, such as shirts and children's toys. Because colors can mean certain things in Chinese culture, I looked carefully at the stores and the items presented for sale and scrutinized the colors. The store walls feature red designs, and there are no completely white spaces (which would represent death). Surrounding the store is a man-made paddling lake of blue water

TABLE 4. Feng shui colors at HKDL

Red: 紅色	Red is the luckiest color, used at Chinese weddings and Chinese New Year celebrations.
White: 白色	White is the color of death, and I could not find any building or space painted white.
Blue: 藍色	Blue is considered a peaceful color that promotes harmony.
Green: 環保	Green is associated with relaxation and serenity.

on which guests can row boats. I saw no green hats, which are said to be worn by a man with an unfaithful wife.[1] Table 4 lists other uses of feng shui colors at HKDL.

Numbers are also important in many Asian traditions. Numerology is the concept that a particular sequence of numbers can bring good or bad luck, and for Chinese people the luck is based on what the number sounds like in Cantonese. HKDL made an interesting attempt to appeal to Asian tourists by constructing a store that sold gold and silver coins with "lucky" combinations of numbers. As I took pictures of the coins, a woman came up to me and showed me the silver coin that I was looking at. She then took out two sheets of paper with many rows of three-digit numbers: some were crossed out, and the salesperson informed me that the coins with those serial numbers were already sold. She said there were only a thousand of these coins and that there were still some lucky numbers left to buy. Confused, I asked, "What do the numbers mean?" She told me that for the coin with 294 on it, 2 stood for "easy, love," 9 stood for "enough," and 4 stood for "lucky." The conversation continued:

JB: What is a good coin souvenir for my mother?
HKDL WORKER: *This* coin is best for your mom because the [serial] number is 839. Eight (八) means long, three (三) means live (sounds like), and nine (九) sounds like rich. That means she will live healthy and long.

82 Fantasies of Hong Kong Disneyland

DRAWING 4. HKDL coin. (Credit: Sally Pirie.)

JB: Which coin for my sister, who has health concerns?
HKDL WORKER: For the health for your sister, I recommend [the coin with the serial number] 498. Four (四) means fortune, nine (九) means enough, and eight (八) means long.
JB: A coin for my husband and myself?
HKDL WORKER: 811—eight (八) means good and eleven (十一) means double love together. All double numbers in Chinese are lucky. It means you will be with the one you love forever and they will love you always.
JB: I'll take the 811.

When I returned to the jewelry store months later, the coins were gone. I was surprised that HKDL had removed what I thought was a sincere and potentially successful indigenization attempt, given the interest of many Asians in numerology. Nonetheless, numbers are important elements

TABLE 5. Feng shui numerology

One: 一個	Associated with wholeness and unity.
Two: 兩	Sounds similar to "sure." Two stands for "doubling up" and for symmetry.
Three: 三個	Sounds like "to live" in Cantonese.
Four: 四個	Sounds like "death" and is considered very unlucky. There are no fourth floors in the HKDL hotels.
Five: 五年	Auspicious especially in combination with two, four, six, or eight.
Six: 六個	Sounds similar to happiness and wealth.
Seven: 七個	Unlucky number, associated with cheating; and July, the seventh month, is inauspicious: "Ghost Month."
Eight: 八個	One of the luckiest numbers, especially in doubles like 88.
Nine: 九	Means completeness and prosperity.
Ten: 十年	Connotes perfection and possibilities.

throughout HKDL, reflecting the belief that numbers can bring positive or negative energies and forces to a person or building. Indeed, HKDL opened on September 12, 2005, because the feng shui consultant whom Disney hired designated this as a providential day to open a business. Many Americans would find this date uncomfortably close to 9/11, but according to the ancient Chinese text *Yi Jing*, September 12 was a propitious date for an opening.

Although HKDL was touted as culturally sensitive for its incorporation of "local" indigenized characteristics such as feng shui, its adherence to feng shui principles is questionable. That the operators of the park were so keen to publicize the feng shui features of the park suggests they wanted to give the impression that the organization was culturally sensitive and sincerely attempting to indigenize a cultural space for Hong Kong people. None of my interviewees, from the workers to the visitors, however, cared about feng shui. Many simply did not know about the existence of any of the elements. This impression is confirmed by Day's (2015) doctoral research, which calls into question some of HKDL's feng shui claims.

On the claim that Hong Kong Disneyland was carefully positioned on Lantau Island in Penny's Bay among the surrounding hills and sea for the best luck, with the lucky feng shui hill formations in the area including the "white tiger" and "green dragon," Day writes that despite a "few token gestures towards *fengshui*, the overall composition of the park is that of a reproduction of the Anaheim USA paradigm" (2015, 257).

OTHER SPATIAL INDIGENIZATION EFFORTS AT HKDL

Disney also attempted to indigenize HKDL through the design of the park's hotels. There are three first-class hotels at HKDL, including the art deco Hollywood Hotel and the Victorian-styled Hong Kong Disneyland Hotel.[2] These hotels demonstrate how Disney has attempted to indigenize to Chinese space norms. Each hotel was built in a carefully selected location with water nearby in a southwesterly direction to maximize prosperity, and each has a feng shui rock in its entrance and courtyard or pool areas. The boulders prevent good fortune from flowing away from the theme park or hotels. Disney claims that the placement of water around these hotels is consistent with good feng shui principles. Day, however, describes this placement as reflecting "standard hotel design and marketing strategies, where hotel rooms with an ocean view are charged at a greater daily tariff than those with no view" (2015, 263). The hotels have multiple floors, but the number four for the fourth floor is nowhere to be seen, because in both Mandarin and Cantonese four is a homonym for death.

Victorian Hotel

There is much to laud about the HKDL Victorian hotel as the architecture is beautiful and the greenery is impressive.

When you check in you are drawn to a six-story lobby that draws you to gaze up through one of the largest windows you have ever seen. Your head is drawn up and you see the greenery and then the blue sky. Walking forward you then see the splendid sea and dock. Disney fans are delighted by the Frozen-themed rooms and palatial grounds. Americans who like California Disneyland may well like the hotel décor and Victorian-customed workers who are trained to say that "Disneyland is all about storytelling." My family enjoyed walking around the hotel with its live band.

The hotel is impressive, but one cannot forget that Hong Kong is one of the most densely packed and expensive urban centers in the world. It boasts one of the highest numbers of Rolls-Royces in the world, while there are also some lower incomed Hong Kongers who live in cages. This space of the hotel and theme park could have been developed to be housing instead of a place that only the transnational elite utilize. It is almost similar to a stadium in the United States or a world event venue where only a few transnational elite can truly utilize it fully. I did not see any locals utilizing the hotel.

Our HKDL Victorian sea balcony hotel room package had so many amenities, including a large pool, sauna, and extravagant buffet meals. We stayed in a sea-view room that had a double-door entry and elaborate Disney-branded fixtures. There was dragon fruit and cake waiting for us in our room and a card that welcomed us. Our Victorian room with a sea balcony was very playful, with French doors that had a childlike crayon drawing on the windows with Disney designs. Everything, from the towels to the slippers, was monogrammed with Disney characters. They provided toothbrushes in seven dwarf containers. There were already chargers and cell phone extension cords in the room waiting for us. Everything had been well thought out beforehand.

When we walked outside our room, Goofy awaited us with a picture-taking opportunity.

Although the concordance of the hotels with feng shui principles is promoted as a good example of Disney's indigenization of the park (Day 2015; Holson 2005a, 2005b), the hotels display no other robust accommodation to Hong Kong culture. The hotels do not engage with any specific location in Hong Kong that could evoke any sort of nostalgic connection to Hong Kong's culture, history, or people.

Edward Said's *Orientalism* (1978) describes a system of thought and beliefs that denote the East or Middle East in particular as inferior to the West. You can see this subordinate depiction of the East through Western texts, literature, and art. He contends that the academy and scholars also justify these depictions. This domination of the East justified colonialization and imperialism. Ultimately Said argues that Orientalism says more about the West or Occident than the East or so-called Orient. Disney being an American western company had Orientalist tendencies in not valuing or depicting anything of Hong Kong origin or culture. The spatial elements of feng shui are invisibilized and limited at best.

Walking around the spatial hallways we noticed sizable Victorian paintings on several walls. There was one sizable Victorianesque painting depicting Asian women and children in Victorian garb in a park that caught our eyes. The painting looked vaguely neo-impressionistic.

From afar we were reminded of the painting *A Sunday Afternoon on the Island of La Grande Jatte* (French: *Un dimanche après-midi à l'Île de la Grande Jatte*) by Georges Seurat. Seurat's masterpiece, estimated to be painted between 1884 and 1886, depicts Parisians at a bucolic park along the River Seine. The HKDL painting shows a similar park scene but with Asian faces. This scene likely never happened in

DRAWING 5. Asian people in Victorian Park. (Credit: Cheynac.)

Hong Kong during this time. In fact, the opposite occurred as there was rioting in Hong Kong in 1884. Lewis Chere highlights that between August 1884 and April 1885 the Sino-French War elicited anti-foreign protests within China. These anti-imperialist protests spread to Hong Kong. The painting of an Asian leisurely family at a Hong Kong park seems to be sanitizing history at best but apocryphal at worst.

There is a total disregard for true Chinese or Hong Kong culture in the hotel's spatial features. While the HKDL Hollywood Hotel is impressive in its construction, it represents a missed opportunity to indigenize Hong Kong culture. Instead of a Hollywood Hotel there should be a Hong Kong Cinema Hotel. Hong Kong is well known for its film industry, with such stars as Bruce Lee and Jackie Chan.

Hong Kong cinema enjoys worldwide fame due to directors Wong Kar-wai, Stephen Chow, and John Woo. If Disney had built a Hong Kong film hotel instead of a Hollywood hotel, this could resonate with Hong Kong locals who yearn to be recognized as having a distinct culture. Hong Kongers yearn for the spaces of a bygone Hong Kong, not those of Main Street USA, a space to which few Hong Kongers have any immediate relationship.

The architecture of the park itself is similarly a missed opportunity to capitalize on nostalgia for Hong Kong's rich and colorful history. Unlike the Hong Kong theme park Ocean Park, which features an Old Hong Kong Land that pays tribute to Hong Kong's heyday in the sixties and seventies, HKDL has no old-time Hong Kong streets that present cultural heritage or evoke nostalgia. Notably absent are the architectural styles of Hong Kong's golden years, such as those displayed at the Hong Kong Museum of History. Hong Kong's architecture has been immortalized in several Western and Eastern films: the setting of the original *Blade Runner* was inspired by Hong Kong skyways, and in the 1980s there was a renaissance of Hong Kong action films depicting a gritty Hong Kong environment. Wong Kar-wai's beautiful urban aesthetic is another example of a stunning use of Hong Kong architecture. In trying to indigenize, Disney could have included these elements. Instead, it created an unusual chimera of architecture that fuses several different cultural backgrounds without evoking Hong Kong's cultural heritage. For instance, HKDL's wishing well (see drawing 6) and several buildings with curved tops seem to evoke Qing dynasty (1644–1912) architecture. Such architecture is found in mainland China in the Old Summer Palace, the Summer Palace, and Qianlong Garden in the Forbidden City.

Just steps away for these structures are modern apartments and future space-age buildings. The choice to feature this type of old Chinese architecture on a wishing well seems anachronistic and vaguely Orientalized. There are many modern architectural styles in both Hong Kong and mainland China. The well has upturned eaves and roof corners, presenting a palimpsest of Orientalism. Chinatowns in the United States hired Anglo architects to build "authentic" Chinese buildings to ward off hostile neighbors who wanted to take over the space.

DRAWING 6. HKDL wishing well. (Credit: Cheynac.)

Another example of an HKDL indigenization attempt in architecture is the Mystic Manor (also called Mystic Point) building (see drawing 7). This structure is a chimera of various architectural styles on top of a Western Disney Haunted House frame. Mystic Manor is colored bright yellow-gold and crimson, with two tones of rich green and bluish-gray rooftops. It is fronted with anachronistic lamps of dark metal in a style that has certainly never been prevalent in Hong Kong. There is a quasi-Japanese archway, but when visitors lift their eyes to the second level, they see a balcony that seems taken from a Western. Next to the balcony is a green wall. The third floor features an imposing faux–Middle

DRAWING 7. HKDL Mystic Manor. (Credit: Cheynac.)

Eastern dome with antennae protruding. When walking up the steps to the Mystic Manor, visitors face yellow (almost golden) gates with a crimson trim; upon arriving at the top, they find two-toned green doors and curved windows colored blue. The colorful Mystic Manor seems to have a colorful overlay on top of the traditional Disney Haunted Mansion.

The manor's ride is intriguing via an adventurous show about a British explorer Lord Mystic and his monkey, Albert. Mystic Manor (迷離大宅) displays the narrative of the eccentric "collectors" who created the original museums. The wonders of the artifacts rely on the exoticization of

DRAWING 8. Victorian nightmare. (Credit: Sally Pirie.)

non-Western cultures. The ride moves through the British collector's home, showing the visitor collections of objects from around the world. The final room is the Chinese Salon, which displays statues and artworks from China. What the ride never mentions is that the collections referenced were largely products of imperialism and conquest rather than fair exchange. The Chinese artifacts at the end may have been an attempt to prove the value of the ride to an Asian guest, but the European colonialist empire theft of the Chinese collection is obscured, including the theft of Hong Kong itself.

It should be noted that the wealth or "treasure" of Europe during this time was built on wide-scale theft of resources from the colonies. Yet another example of missed indigenization is found in Mystic Point's Garden of Wonders, an archaeological site full of three-dimensional figures. For example, the Lasmassu Bas-Relief is "three segments of an ancient carving [that] form a celestial being from Mesopotamian mythology, the Lamassu. Together they are arranged in such a manner to provide a forced perspective optical illusion for photo opportunities."[3] The garden does *not* feature such Chinese archaeological finds as Terracotta Army soldiers or miniature examples of wonders such as the Great Wall. It also lacks any figures local to Hong Kong, such as neolithic Hong Kong artifacts or relics from Hong Kong's recent fishing boat past.

No Utopia for Visitors: A "Budget Theme Park"

From most visitors' perspective, such indigenization attempts are far from sufficient to produce an enjoyable park experience. For them, a successful park needs above all to provide appealing, high-quality rides and other attractions. It is relevant, then, that HKDL is the smallest Disneyland park in the world. At the time HKDL was built, the Walt Disney Company was simultaneously building several other theme parks and running out of money (Defunctland 2019). The loss of leadership when Disney CEO Michael Eisner resigned on September 30, 2005, caused further disruption. HKDL therefore became a "budget theme park" with undeveloped spaces and few attractions (Defunctland 2019). A normal Disneyland park has twice as many attractions as HKDL. According to the documentary Defunctland HKDL has even counted nonattractions as attractions to make the park seem more appealing. Among the original twenty-two attractions counted were City Hall, guest relations, vehicles on Main Street, and tiki statues that squirt water; even the railroad, with just one stop, was counted as an attraction. This suggests that Disney avoided any elaborate and expensive theming that would have involved building many new rides, choosing instead to install a bare-bones "frontierland" theme that required no rides and presents as open spaces fitting the theme. Themed open spaces, such as the largely bare frontierlands at HKDL, cost much less than rides (Defunctland 2019, 8:23). Disney could perhaps argue that it was evoking a utopian image of the Western past, but the fact remains that numerous HKDL visitors have complained about the lack of rides.

Many of the buildings at HKDL display surface-level changes meant to fix poorly conceived buildings. One example is the new Magical Dreams Castle, with the same hodgepodge of architecture built on top of the original structure. It now has multiple princesses shown in strong poses. The castle uses elements from several design traditions, melding together gold domes with European-inspired roofs. Elissaveta Brandon writes, "The result is a palimpsest of sorts, where versions of many castles—the California original, Hong Kong's 2005 replica and the brand-new Castle of Magical Dreams—come together as one. After the multiyear, 10.9 billion Hong Kong dollar ($1.4 billion) expansion, which also saw the park welcome multiple new attractions, the re-imagined castle is over twice the height of the old one" (Brandon 2021).

Another architectural feature at HKDL is the Sleeping Beauty Castle, now the Magical Dreams Castle. The original Sleeping Beauty Castle was a copy of the structure at Disneyland in California, but it was small and underwhelming; it felt shallow and lacking when compared to other global Disneyland castles. In 2016, the castle was expanded: "To honor its founder's vision, Disney decided to preserve Hong Kong's Sleeping Beauty Castle when it embarked on a major expansion in 2016—instead of demolishing it entirely, designers built atop and around it" (Brandon 2021). The new castle features a number of female characters from Disney movies, such as Belle. Because it was built on the 2005 base, the new castle is a palimpsest of different castles; it is certainly taller, but I expect that Hong Kong visitors would prefer more rides, stores, and attractions to taller buildings. Building on top of an unimpressive castle is an example of yet another low-budget transformation.

HKDL as Dystopia

The analysis in the preceding sections has demonstrated that Disney's attempts at indigenizing the space of HKDL have been incomplete or ineffective at best and expressions of Orientalism at worst. But Disney's efforts to make the park a utopia have been undercut not just by its failed indigenization but also by the history of the land on which the park is built and the impact of the park on its environment. To make more room for buildings, parts of Hong Kong are built on land reclaimed from the harbor, with part of the ocean floor paved over. HKDL was built on land reclaimed from Penny Bay. While dredging the ocean floor to remove debris, a large number of World War II bombs were discovered. Similar bombs had been found in Hong Kong in the past, as the dredgers work "in waters used as a dumping ground by the

British military for decades" (Associated Press 2001). In the case of HKDL, bomb disposal experts said that they would not be able to find all of the bombs on the site and that the theme park would therefore be built on unexploded World War II bombs. Although the bombs are inactive and there is little chance of an explosion, the presence of these bombs is a testament to Hong Kong's colonial past.

When entering HKDL, visitors pass a metal Mickey Mouse figure surfing on a metal whale. To borrow Baudrillard's terminology, this figure is a simulacrum, an image of something that was not real to begin with. However, real animals were killed so that the Disney animals could be built and displayed to visitors. During the construction of the park, news reports emerged of feral dogs being used as guard dogs by the construction workers. The workers disputed that these dogs were being used in this way; nevertheless, forty-five dogs were captured and more than forty were euthanized (*BBC News* 2005). One can surmise that they were not the only animal victims of the construction, as most of the wildlife on the site would have died when the ocean was paved over to accommodate the theme park. When a small group of environmentalists protested over all of the fish that were being killed, Disney responded that the amount of dead fish was normal and to be expected (*BBC News* 2005).

Another dystopian element of HKDL is the alleged contribution of its fireworks displays to air pollution. Hong Kong already has significant pollution because of its proximity to the factories of Guangzhou. The nightly fireworks show at HKDL has been highly controversial for its contribution to air pollution: "In August 2005, complaints also arose because Disney was not planning to use the more environmentally friendly air-launch technology for its fireworks in Hong Kong as they were in other parks, such as in Anaheim" (Hills and Welford 2006, 51, quoted in Mittermeier

DRAWING 9. Dead fish. (Credit: Sally Pirie.)

2021, 159). At Anaheim Disneyland, local activists have claimed that the nightly fireworks are highly polluting and have caused an increase in asthma among local children. Californian activist groups have successfully gotten Disney to stop using some of the most polluting and carcinogenic fireworks at Anaheim Disneyland. It is alleged that these fireworks, now banned at Disneyland in California, are being put to use every night at HKDL.

Conclusion

In my interviews, many visitors expressed indifference about the attempts at indigenization through feng shui. My interviewees indicated that HKDL's spatial indigenization was of no interest to them; one said that it was just for the benefit of the business and did not affect her (interview, HKDL laborer, 2010). And the coin store, which appeared to be a sincere attempt to focus on numerology, has been shut down. Hong Kong could have been the ideal setting for a *heterotopia* that could welcome guests from Hong Kong, greater China, and foreign countries. Ultimately, however, HKDL's space indigenization must be considered a failure. There were many missed opportunities to deeply incorporate Hong Kong Culture into HKDL such as art, food, and hotels. The HKDL hotel did have events like Tai Chi with Goofy, which were very whimsical and family friendly. The Victorian Hong Kong hotel food was very expansive and delicious. Although Disney attempted to indigenize by hiring a feng shui master and in other ways, the local people were not impressed and the attempts seem superficial.

4

An Indigenous Competitor

Ocean Park

Ding ding ding ding! As I approach the doors of the MTR Subway South Island Line, I hear an automated announcement: "Please stand back from the platform door." It is repeated in English, Cantonese, and Mandarin. The platform is crowded with locals, tourists with colorful wheeled luggage, and workers scurrying about.

Ding ding ding ding! I look down and see the words "Please mind the gap" (請小心月台空隙) *along with two white arrows slanted on the far right and left. The arrows show how to enter the train. A green arrow in the middle points straight out, signifying that those exiting have the right of way. I walk in.*

Ding ding ding! The MTR door closes, and I sit down on one of the ultra-clean MTR metal seats as we leave for Ocean Park.

The door opens, and my family and I walk through the station and up the escalator to the exit B. Outside, we see the huge Ocean Park sign with a seal waving at us in the background. In the middle is a captain seal named Whiskers in a French sailor outfit. His red bandana, smile, and fin entice us in.

FIGURE 9. Cable car view. (Photo courtesy of Sean Slusser.)

We walk up to the cable car, which takes passengers from the waterfront to the summit and back, crossing over the water. The roaring of the engines make me put my hands on both my ears. We get in line to enter our own transparent yellow cable car, which is held up by interconnecting metal cables. The screeching of metal on metal is loud, and our cable car suddenly drops into the other metal cables and whisks us into the open air. My heart drops as we start to move across the sky, so high above the sea. I look at the unending views of the bay, hills, and the South China Sea (南中國海).

My breath catches as we morph into Spirited Away soot mites. . . .

We are beginning a liminal journey between sky and sea, floating through the surrounding clouds. I see my daughter's eyes widen and she gasps, "I feel like a bird flying in a Studio Ghibli movie!" We glide to the other side slowly and without speaking, as nature is deafening us with its divinity. Our eyes cannot widen any more. There are Treebeard's descendants in the green hills below. Ponyo is in the unending sea waving at us. Haku is majestically flying next to us through the clouds as we transform into Shikigami tiny bird-shaped papers. Our names are forgotten and our souls are finally free.

Our metal cable car bubble floats us to the other side all too soon. We hear the shrieking sound of metal colliding with metal, loud engine sounds shutting off as we connect with the platform. The doors open, and our feet suddenly sink into the ground as we become terrestrial beings again. My eyes are puffy and my face has streaks that I smooth over with my hand. My nose is runny as I stutter out the words, "Hong Kong's nature is beautiful" (field notes July 10, 2023).

To conclude this study, this chapter shows how a different park has successfully indigenized in the areas where Hong Kong Disneyland failed. This concluding chapter argues that Ocean Park (OP) is better indigenized to Hong Kong people than HKDL in the three key areas examined in this book: space, labor, and consumption. OP is a homegrown amusement park—a locally owned and nonprofit theme park, zoo, and aquarium. Unlike HKDL, OP is agile and responsive, and it presents a culturally competent Hong Kong theme park experience. It offers a specifically Hong Kong brand of nostalgia, in contrast to HKDL,

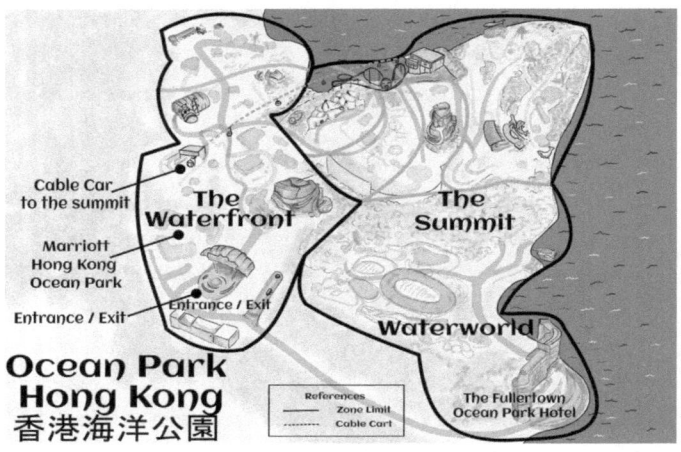

MAP 2. Ocean Park. (Credit: Viviana Moyano)

which offers an American nostalgia. Moreover, OP is designed to take advantage of Hong Kong's natural beauty. It draws on a primarily local workforce, and it is generally cheaper than HKDL. Unsurprisingly, many Hong Kong residents prefer it to HKDL.

Many people predicted that OP would be forced to close when HKDL arrived. Instead, multiple people fought to revive and sustain this marine theme park. Two key OP executives, Allan Zeman and Tom Mehrmann, used their unique expertise to help OP to transform, survive, and thrive. They did this by demonstrating extraordinary skill and respect for the local Hong Kong people and community. They respectfully listened to the local community and incorporated what they wanted while also modernizing the park to Western global tastes. These two individuals could see the uniqueness of what Hong Kong could offer. Hong Kongers were delighted and attended in droves. As a result, OP has outperformed HKDL in attendance for over a decade.

Ocean Park: Background

On January 10, 1977, Sir Murray MacLehose, governor of Hong Kong, opened Ocean Park. The Hong Kong government donated the land where it was built. The Hong Kong Jockey Club built it for HK$150 million. Between 1982 and 1984, the Jockey Club allocated an additional HK$240 million to fund the park's second phase of development, which included adding attractions with the intention of increasing profits and making full use of the land. In addition, OP does work in both fauna and flora conservation. It runs a notable breeding program and features enclosures where visitors can see rare animals such as sharks, birds, and dolphins. In 1993 OP established the Ocean Park Conservation Foundation, and in 1999 it established the Hong Kong Society for Panda Conservation. In 2005 the two groups merged into the Ocean Park Conservation Foundation Hong Kong, whose mission is to use service, research, and educational advocacy to support Asian conservation efforts.

Today, Ocean Park is a government-owned nonprofit entity devoted to entertainment, education, and conservation. Its mission is to give guests experiences that are enjoyable, compelling, and informative (Ocean Park Corporation 2023). OP is not a franchise; instead, it was established and developed by the people of Hong Kong for the people of Hong Kong. This is notable as it is not a cookie-cutter copy or transnational.

Space Indigenization

Hong Kong is one of the most overpopulated places in the world. The city contains extreme inequalities, with both great poverty and intensely concentrated wealth. Hong Kong is known as an advanced international financial center rather than a city of natural beauty.

Amid this urban environment, the stunningly beautiful Ocean Park is a green oasis. It is located in the south district of Hong Kong and consists of two main areas: the Waterfront and the Summit. It has seven attraction zones: Amazing Asian Animals, Aqua City, Marine World, Whiskers Harbour, Polar Adventure, Thrill Mountain, and the Rainforest. A giant, transparent, bubble-shaped cable car makes visitors feel as though they are floating in the air as they travel from the lowland area to the headland through the fog. The scenery is otherworldly, filled with Hong Kong's mountains, sea, and hills.

Ocean Park houses an astounding number of Asian animals in various exhibits. It is the largest marine-based theme park in Asia and the only Asian park to be accredited by the American Zoo and Aquarium Association (Yim 2010, 207–209). In 2009, OP launched a HK$5.55 billion master redevelopment program that involved rare Asian animals. It also launched a limited-edition Red Stamp pack to help earthquake reconstruction in panda habitats in Sichuan, China.

OP is a leader in interactive animal education and nature conservation. Nature educators provide daily animal fun talks to promote conservation. One popular attraction is the park's pandas, all of which are owned by mainland China. In 2009, red pandas with burnished fur arrived at OP (Tsang 2023b). OP guests can see these rare animals in the Giant Panda Adventure, an indoor-outdoor exhibit. OP also has a rare sloth that comes out infrequently but is an enchanting treat when it does appear. Other popular animals include penguins, seals, sharks, and jellyfish.

Headland Rides and Adventureland is where a visitor can hear screams from roller-coaster riders. Unlike HKDL's fairly tame rides, OP's rides are fast and scary enough to appeal to teenagers. But to fully appreciate OP's indigenization, we must turn to the Old Hong Kong area. The entrance features a bright-red sign that reads "Old Hong Kong." The architecture of the space presents a nostalgic vision of Hong Kong of the fifties to seventies. It features *tong lau* 唐樓, mixed-use tenement buildings once common in Hong Kong, Taiwan, Southeast Asia, and Southern China. Although they no longer exist in HK, someone who has lived in HK for a long time would likely recognize these structures.

Old Hong Kong Alleyways

The Old Hong Kong alleyways are decorated with bird cages, hanging clothes, and medicine shops, with vintage posters along the walls depicting a Hong Kong that no longer exists. Old Hong Kong also includes a vintage "heritage tram" and old street signs, and it offers authentic street food from food stalls. A theater is a central attraction: it once held live shows of the beloved pig character McDull 麦兜, an iconic and quintessentially Hong Kong cartoon. Old Hong Kong delivers a nostalgic past, characterized by a calmer pace and a communal, collectivist spirit from the era before the industrialization of the city. Whereas Hong Kong Disneyland seems designed to evoke nostalgia for a foreign land, the American West, Old Hong Kong delivers a culturally relevant nostalgia that has appealed to generations of local Hong Kong guests.

Hong Kong is known to be quite a modern space in comparison to other Asian places and even those within China. It is known for its many skyscrapers and malls. These metal building did not always dominate the skyline, as it was once a thriving fishing boat community. There was a lot of communal living in cramped conditions. The film *Echoes of the Rainbow* (2010), directed by Alex Law, depicts a 1960s

DRAWING 10. McDull in Old Time Hong Kong Area in Ocean Park. (Credit: Sally Pirie.)

British Hong Kong that enjoyed much mutual aid community among neighbors. But those old 1960s buildings were torn down and replaced. The fishing family places were paved over and large-scale housing was built. Many old city landmarks and buildings were destroyed to make way for "progress" and racial capitalism.

Labor Indigenization

Over the nearly fifty years since OP opened, thousands of workers—mostly Hong Kong locals—have worked there. Those people on the ground have likely had a huge impact on the success of OP, although we cannot list their names or quantify their efforts. We do know the names of the CEOs and chairmen who have also contributed to OP's success. To illustrate OP's labor indigenization, here I highlight two of these leaders, chairman Tom Mehrmann (2004–2016) and

CEO Allan Zeman (2003–2014). At a time when onlookers were predicting that OP would shut down, Mehrmann and Zeman led an innovation project to help the park survive. Tung Chee Hwa, first chief executive and president of the Hong Kong Executive Council, tapped Zeman to be the chairman of the Ocean Park Board. Zeman, a Canadian national who later gained Chinese citizenship, was responsible for the park's mission, its board of directors, and strategic planning. *Forbes* (2007) magazine dubbed him the "Mouse Killer" because he made Ocean Park very successful while HK Disney floundered. (Outside Ocean Park, he had developed the Lan Kwai Fong district in Central, Hong Kong, which is enjoyed by expats and locals alike.) His out-of-the-box approaches made OP successful. He famously dressed up as a jellyfish for a viral marketing stunt. Zeman broke the rules by saying he was going to develop three OP hotels, something he did not have governmental permission to say. He later developed two of the hotels. He professionalized the workers by having them wear new uniforms and redeveloped many of OP's attractions and added new ones. According to Collins (2017), "Zeman oversaw a HK$5.5 billion revamp of Ocean Park Theme Park between 2006 and 2012 and it is now one of the ten most visited theme parks in the world, consistently outperforming Disney locally. His efforts were internationally recognized when Ocean Park won the Applause Award—the highest international accolade in the theme park industry in 2013." Table 6 illustrates Zeman's vision for OP's values in contrast to what he perceived as HKDL's values.

Zeman handpicked Thomas Mehrmann, a longtime theme park executive, to be the park's CEO. Mehrmann had over twenty years of leadership and development experience at Knott's Berry Farm, Mall of America, and Six Flags Marine World and was known as a proponent of honoring

TABLE 6. Ocean Park's and Hong Kong Disneyland's values, compared

Ocean Park	Hong Kong Disneyland
Hong Kong culture	American culture
Generational values and memories as Hong Kong People's Park	Generational values and memories as American People's Park
HK Jockey Club donated park to Hong Kong people	Walt Disney's midwestern dreams
Nonprofit	Profit for shareholders
Cable car	Castle
Iconic attractions: cable car, aquarium, and Asian Halloween	Iconic attraction: It's a Small World
Whiskers and friends: Turtle, Artic Fox, Panda Bear, Sharks, Seal Lion, Jellyfish	Duffy the Disney Bear is Mickey Mouse's own teddy bear. Duffy friends: Gelatoni, StellaLou, CookieAnn, and Olu Mel
Nature	Movies
Conservation classes for Hong Kong kids	Grants, donations to various programs

SOURCE: Ocean Park Corporation (2021b, 2023); Mehrmann and Switow (2018, 56).

and building the local community. According to a 2016 article, he worked at the park seven days a week, making himself "accessible" to its employees (Nip 2016). In *Taming the Mouse: How a Small Hong Kong Theme Park Came to Dominate Disney* (2018), which Mehrmann coauthored with Michael Switow, he describes how the park was able to outmaneuver HKDL to achieve higher attendance numbers for ten straight years (see figure 10). Describing the principles he relied on to realize this success, he explains that he had to understand OP first and then seek to be understood (27); that OP had to adhere to its core values, expressed in the company's vision and mission; and that OP had to differentiate itself from other attractions: "We need to complement Disney; not compete with them" (53). When Mehrmann came to OP, he jump-started the planning process for the park. He also emphasized that OP had to be culturally relevant to its visitors, 35 to 45 percent of whom are Hong Kong

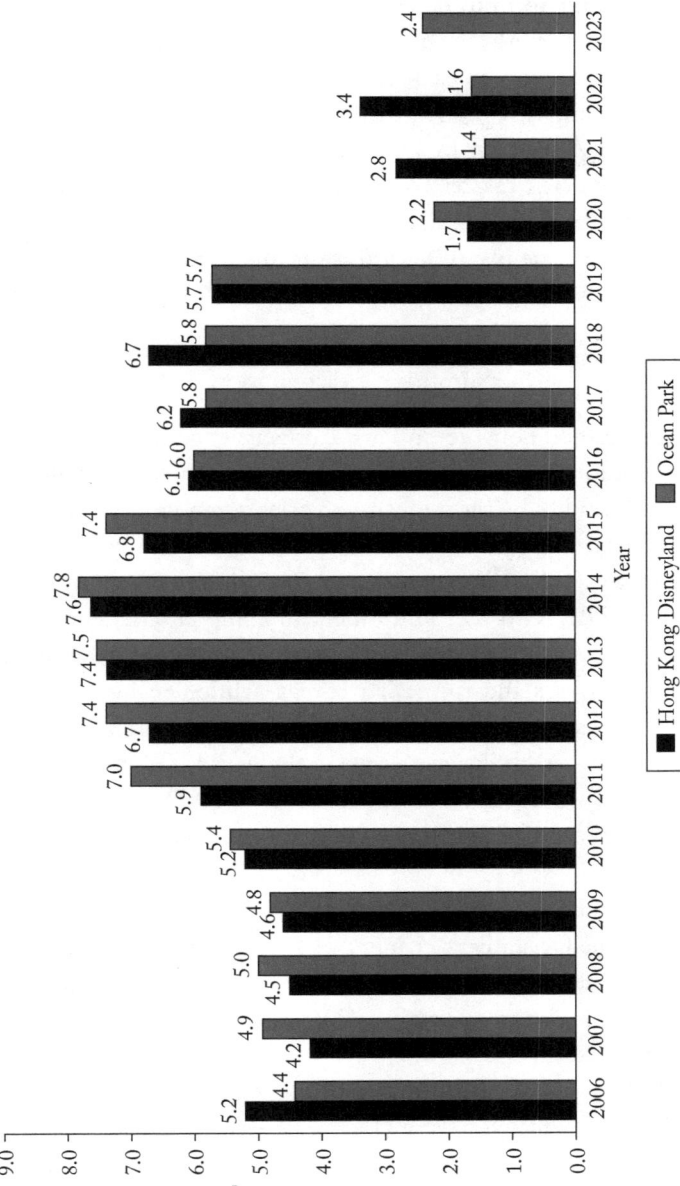

FIGURE 10. Hong Kong Disneyland and Ocean Park attendance 2006–2023. Sources: Hong Kong Disneyland (2006–2022), Ocean Park Corporation (2006–2023). (Credit: Pedram Maymand.)

residents and 40 to 50 percent of whom are mainland Chinese visitors, with the rest coming from other parts of Asia (116). He led by example, being present and catching workers doing things right (141). He created disruptive marketing for Aqua City by introducing a unique song, a viral video, and other masterful public relations (176). These two executives' synergy and respect for the local Hong Kong cultural heritage played a significant role in making Ocean Park successful again.

Consumption Indigenization

To understand how Ocean Park tailors its experience to the tastes of local visitors, consider its Halloween celebration, which is said to be the largest such celebration in the world. OP is well-known for its Halloween events with haunted attractions. This celebration is more terrifying than anything that HKDL, with its commitment to being child-friendly, can offer. According to Mehrmann, "We set up 8 eight haunted houses and run 13 live shows, while 666 monsters roam the park during a six week. That attracts more visitors than any other Halloween event in the world" (Mehrmann and Switow 2018, 45). The appeal of OP's Halloween celebration was confirmed by one of my interviewees:

JB: What do you think about Ocean Park?
CHANG: The Ocean Park Haunted Night—It is really scary! It is not intended for kids. It is really scary—the area is quite big—it is always sold out—and it has been going on for ten years.
JB: Do Hong Kongers like it?
CHANG: It is targeted toward HK people—the taste and style. It is not an American Halloween. Ocean Park has Asian ghosts. (interview, HK resident, 2009)

To create the Halloween celebration, Ocean Park surveyed locals about their views of the originally Western holiday. They found that Hong Kongers were amused by Western ghost images but were scared of Cantonese ghost stories. After listening to his local staff, Mehrmann approved the use of terrifying Hong Kong Cantonese haunted houses and stories: "My marketing team approached me at the time with the storyboard of a commercial they wanted to run: a young boy is playing outside his housing estate near a squeaky carousel. He stands there, his foot on top of a soccer ball, gazing into space like something is possessing him. His mother approaches and shakes him. (This is all done in black and white, with eerie lighting.) When his mother finally wakes him from the trance, he says Papa!" (Mehrmann and Switow 2018, 46). According to a Cantonese saying, Mehrmann's marketing director told him, you can be so frightened that you forget your mother's name. Mehrmann also learned that the Hong Kong market demanded a new haunted house each year, unlike the Disneyland model that produces the same haunted house yearly.

Ocean Park also incorporates local cartoons into its programming. Most notably, in the Old Hong Kong area there is a cinema that (at least prior to the COVID-19 pandemic) showed the classic Hong Kong cartoon McDull and McMug, and the park offers McDull-themed dishes for guests to eat. McDull and McMug are kindergarten-aged piglets created in the 1980s by Brian Tse and Alice Mak. According to Sotheby's, "McDull and his cousin McMug have a special significance to those who grew up in Hong Kong. Since the 1980s, when the cartoon duo first appeared in Ming Pao Children's Weekly, they have been and still are an essential part of childhood" (Sotheby's 2022). McDull and McMug live in poverty and find adventures throughout Hong Kong. These excruciatingly cute, fat-faced piglets with big pink snouts are not particularly brilliant, talented, or special, but they both delight in wonder. They try and fail and try again, and dream with big imaginations. Children can look to McDull as a symbol of making the best of their mistakes, while adults can see the bittersweet pursuits of life in Hong Kong, restricted by the competitive capitalist realities of the city. The humor of McDull relies on an intensely local humor that only the Hong Konger Cantonese audience can understand, characterized by the exceedingly long Cantonese rhyming insults, rapid-fire staccato Cantonese words, exaggerated legato sounds, and long silences. Ocean Park's collaboration with McDull the pig offers entertainment that resonates with locals who have lived similar lives growing up in the busy city. The characters of Minnie and Mickey do not evoke the same nostalgic feelings of defeat, wonder, and joy as the beloved distinctly Hong Kong piglet.

In the area of food, Ocean Park offers some third-party Western foods such as McDonald's hamburgers and fries, but the park has made a conscious effort to offer more local food options than in the past, focusing on quality and local flavors. Guests can buy meals at low-priced *dai pai dong* (simplified Chinese: 大牌档; traditional Chinese: 大牌檔; pinyin: dàpáidàng), open-air food stalls. This is notable as many of these outdoor food stalls were pushed indoors by the government. They can also eat at a *cha chaan teng* (茶餐廳), a Hong Kong–style cafe or diner, or the Panda Café, which focuses on Sichuan and Hong Kong specialties. These restaurants typically offer large menus of Hong Kong–style Western foods like toast with peanut butter and macaroni soup with ham. A Chinese sit-down restaurant that specializes in Cantonese food is another option. The themes are variety, low prices, and high-quality food, in keeping with the Hong Kong tradition of enjoying delicious food that is accessibly priced. Mehrmann played a pivotal role in many of these indigenization efforts.

Conclusion

Hong Kong Disneyland claimed it was culturally relevant when it opened in 2005. However, in preparation for opening the park, Disney conducted focus groups that only superficially illuminated the core local market's needs. As this book has shown, Disney failed to indigenize in several key areas. It is true that HKDL has continued to innovate and has improved its offerings significantly, especially in its highlighting of the Duffy and Friends CookieAnn collection. It is also true that the creation of Hong Kong Disneyland spurred the older Ocean Park theme park to innovate, redesign, and build. Ultimately Ocean Park does a much better job at indigenizing to the local Hong Kong community by innovating and having significant leadership that is sustained and considerate of the local community. Ultimately OP needs HKDL to survive and prosper as they are tied together. Both OP and HKDL are also tied to the Hong Kong tourism industry and its ebbs and flows. OP wants and needs Disney to be successful, and maybe the future will bring collaborations such as the issuance of two-park tickets. The more tourists HKDL draws in, the more chances Ocean Park will have to succeed at its highest levels. Many things have significantly changed in Hong Kong because of the global pandemic and also the political situation with the new unpopular laws. These laws are spurring some Hong Kongers to move abroad. Many will not come back. This outmigration trend is still being tracked and monitored and is part of a large pattern of people coming and going from Hong Kong. HK people have always fought for themselves. They do not want to be just another Chinese city and believe they have a unique contribution. HK had many Western corporations leave, but it still has a bigger infrastructure of expatriates than other Asian cities.

Visions of Hong Kong

It is dark and my family is waiting for the water show. I don't want to leave, because I don't know how many years it will take me to get back to Hong Kong. The end of the night at Ocean Park includes "Visions of Hong Kong," a dramatic light and water show. The show begins with thick fog and water shooting into the sky. A woman is projected with swinging arms, pushing light around her, sending forth an image of the Chinese neon signs and iconic Hong Kong skyline behind her. Projections of dolphins and fish dance across the water with flashing blue and purple lights. A Chinese opera figure emerges with long white flowing sleeves, paired with Chinese opera instrumentals. She disappears, and fire spurts along to the drums. Depictions of the opera performer's face are shown on the building, with a white face, smoky eyes, and traditional Chinese opera headdress. Majestic cranes then fly across the building behind a flowing waterfall. The music softens, the lights change to warm tones, and sparkles go across the building with magical water displays. The second half of the show displays a friendly octopus figure that hugs the building, highlighting the wildlife of the park. The octopus changes into a flapping bird with colorful feathers. Then the octopus returns, wiggling its tentacles to the enchanting music. The show highlights a vision of Hong Kong that incorporates both local nostalgia for opera performers and the Hong Kong wildlife currently featured in the park. These buoyant images look to Hong Kong's future with hope.

Epilogue

This book took me fifteen years from start to finish, and as I type these words, I know it will become a cultural artifact of a snapshot in time. I shed a lot of tears over this, and it was not easy for a gal with eighth-grade-educated Chinese-Vietnamese restaurant worker parents to produce.

There were many hospital visits because of this book.

Half my body was paralyzed periodically over deep fears, which made me lose my ability to walk for twenty-four hours a few times. Doing fieldwork with a then–history grad student husband, preschooler, and second grader was complicated, but I have distinct intergenerational advantages. My ancestors are in my bone marrow and defend me when need be. My family grew up with this book. I had to fight so many demons, and I was scared that people would come for me.

HK people do not come for me!

I do not have imposter syndrome as my parents or maybe my ancestors made me an instrument for my people. I love my all Hong Kong, Chinese, and Asian folks. All Asians are my 家 (jiā). This story is full of ambiguities. My core argument is that HKDL attempted indigenization to uneven results in space, labor, and consumption. OP, their local competitor or compatible fictive partner, has done a better job at indigenizing. No polemics.

There's more to the story.

There were more pages here that I could not write about. Due to a misunderstanding, I lost my hearing for a day after I saw sweatshop factory pictures of missing limbs. I could not walk from the stress after some interviews. One of my Hong Kong interviewees told me the people she hated the most were the Indo-China "boat people" refugees who came in the 1970s.

Wait, was she talking about my Sino-descended family?

She was, but I wear the mask of *American modernity* bolstered by a PhD that masks my working-class background. My Catholic school background makes me acceptable in some academic circles, but I always feel uncomfortable in these spaces. I am uncomfortable writing these paragraphs. I am uncomfortable now being a part of the Asian people but also apart from Asian people. The space between two words is an ocean.

Does that even make sense?

I was told to quit this book several times, but I could not let it go. It was a shadow in my brain and I felt a lot of stress, guilt, and shame over it. The fear was real to me, and I felt a lack of community as no one is like me. Why can't I publish as fast or as often as others? My parents are not professors but instead semi-literate rough-handed Chinese restaurant workers. As my uncle says, "I [we] have an accent in every language we speak" (Banh 2019a). Dr. Gabor Mate says he was "driven by unconscious needs to validate his existence," so he overworked for years, missing out on family time. Is this book my validation for being?

HK people do not come for me!

Driven to get those Catholic school white ribbons and avoid the mass spankings in class when anyone talked has always been my goal. Hong Kong is my world. Disney has always been in my dreams. Fantasyland. People are magic, and I thought this was a funny story to tell my students and fellow anthro professors about a liminal place that continues to fight. In Barbara Myerhoff's *Number Our Days* (1980), Holocaust survivor Shmuel Goldman says, "We fight to keep warm," and so I recorded just a story of HK people fighting to keep warm.

Don't give up Hong Kong!

> *You.*
> > *Are.*
> > > *Rare.*

Born out of racial capitalism and colonialization;

> *You*
> > *Have*
> > > *Survived.*

HKDL, OP and Hong Kong people must fight to keep warm.

Fight.
Fight.
Fight.

DRAWING 11. Forever playing in the Enchanted Forest. Adapted from A. A. Milne, *The House at Pooh Corner* (1928). (Credit: Alyssa Wu.)

I was scared about every sentence I wrote, but my student Brandon says undergraduate students don't read full paragraphs anymore and only the first sentences of paragraphs. Yes, so good that you students have missed everything traumatic and funny that I have written. Well, those spaces between the first and last sentences were immense, but the spaces between the sentences are bigger than the whole world.

I swear I am a bigger fan of Kendrick Lamar than Taylor Swift.

It is the omissions that is the other story. More important perhaps? I am not the one to write that other story. Find out about the Hong Kong that I could not show. Beyond the Wong Kar-wai, *Chungking Express*, and Bruce Lee fetishizations.

I'm sad
this will be my first and maybe last book

as it took too much out of me.

Like Frodo going on this journey changed me. After this I never get to play with Minnie, Mulan, CookieAnn, or McDull again. I left HK when I was three months old and never had toys or any birthday parties as my parents were just in survival mode in Belleview, Illinois. But I finally got to go back to Hong Kong when I was eighteen after I got into UCLA and my parents took us there for a graduation trip. I plotted and plotted to go back one day, and this book was my masterplan to stay there a bit longer.

Where we go, wherever we do, you, little me, and our toy friends in the Enchanted Forest will always be playing together.[1]

Postscript

Fairytale Endings

I still can't say goodbye

Imagining new worlds now so now I call out to you dear reader, geeks, students, Disney fanatics, and new friends. We need to have more people write, critique, produce, and learn about Asian America and Asia.

Polycentrism.

Ethnic studies needs allies, coconspirators, and friends. I like the convergences of pop culture and Asian America and its diaspora.

But reader, what do you like?

We need more people to consume Asian culture and know its history and diversity. Asian American and Asian studies have very different theoretical frameworks and origins. These fields can be foes and friends, so you should learn the contentious differences. Both sides are suspicious of me in different ways.

They should be.

This "consumption" should be deep, respectful, and reciprocal and include the artist and Asian community in dialogue. Give them the credit that they are due and do not replace and displace them. Bruce Lee, for the television show *Green Hornet*, was paid US$400 while his costars made over US$2,000. This book is about Hong Kong and American consumption of each other and its problematics.

Asians aren't disposable, replaceable, and they won't be silenced.

So, I make a call to you to read more books on Asian America and Asia. Tell people about Asian American books and assign them in class. Learn about the "Secret War." Experience Asian excellence but also know that they are just humans like you with plenty of good and bad.

Asians are human.

Édouard Glissant says everyone, especially colonialized people, has "the right to opacity." Go to eat at Chinese restaurants, shop Indian grocery stores, listen to K-pop, watch Bollywood films, and support Asian American creatives. Traveling to Asia is a step, but living there is even better. #StopAsianHate #SupportChineseRestaurants

If you are a student, consider majoring, or minoring in Asian American and Asian studies, double majoring in this field. Your parents will be happy that you are getting a two for one. If they don't have it then start a petition and contact me for help. No, you do not have to be Asian to get an Asian American and Asian studies major or minor. I took four African American classes while at UCLA and I should have gotten the Africana minor to show that Black Lives Matter. I am a recipient of endless Black love and mentorship, which is part of a long history of Afro-Asian solidarities.

DRAWING 12. Spreading Asian joy and love. Won't say goodbye. (Credit: Sally Pirie.)

All of America is supported by the invisible labor of African Americans and other people of color that makes us function. This global neoliberal machine takes and takes from Black culture while simultaneously demoting, invisibilizing, and exploiting Black people. Edward Said's *Orientalism* remains relevant today.

So I call on you to support ethnic and women's studies in all ways.

My students, staff and faculty are in a tailspin of despair.
Everyone feels tired.
Me too.
But we gotta fight to keep warm.

Stay longer with me.

We must uplift each other with arts, community service, nature, meditation, and movement. I write this at the tail end of the COVID-19 pandemic amidst numerous anti-Asian hate crimes, #StopAsianHate, and the only way I can fight back is with this book, which is intended to *Spread Asian Joy and Love*.

再见 *(goodbye/see you again)*

Acknowledgments

I would like to thank my blind peer reviewers, as their feedback was invaluable and improved the quality of this book tremendously. I would like to thank all the interviewees over the past fifteen years and the UCLA Labor Grant. I could not have finished this book without a California State University, Fresno sabbatical. Jayne Jones got me to write my first page after years of not feeling confident, and Kali Handelman gave me very gentle editorial feedback. AsiaEdit.com edited the grammar, and Allison Van Deventer's expert developmental editing took me to the completion of this book. I am also grateful to Katelyn E. Knox for her writing system programs. The writing spiritual advisors sent me their positive energy so I could access source energy: Deborah Harlow, Namrata Kokal, Jack Ji, Margarita Escalante, and Kristin Dwan. Your healing voices are in my soul, and you have healed me greatly.

I greatly appreciate Rick Rubin's 2023 book *The Creativity Act*, which I read multiple times and colored and highlighted each page. Taylor Swift and Kendrick Lamar helped me with their lyrics. Nina Simone's fighting spirit is always in my heart.

This book project would not have been possible without Rutgers University Press associate press director and editorial director Kimberly Guinta, who had me do monthly check-ins that really kicked in my internal Catholic schoolgirl. I had to please Ms. Kimberly! Her confidence in the book really affected me. She did not give up on me. How do you thank someone who changed your life? I also want to thank Rutgers editors Carah Naseem and Emma-Li Downer, who were professional, concise, kind, and very encouraging. Thanks go to Daryl Brower at Rutgers, Sherry Gerstein at Westchester Publishing Services, and Joseph Dahm, my copyeditor, as well.

Good leadership is crucial to the health of organizations, and I am lucky to have extremely forward-thinking leaders who are brilliant, gracious, and kind: Elizabeth Lowham, Jennifer Randles, and Dvera Saxton. Elizabeth again and again championed our Social Science college, and I am so deeply grateful for her leadership. I would also like to thank Michelle Denbeste and Yoshiko Takahashi, who support research scholars. Franklin Ng and Katsuyo Howard dropped seeds for forty years before I got to this university, and so I sit under the shade of the forest they made. Haiming Lui has been my supportive colleague my entire academic career.

Very few people on earth can understand how you have to fight all your demons to write a university press book along with rejection, humiliation, and fear. My writing buddies had the same fight, and I am grateful for these randomly met fellow academic warriors who were also writing first books: Taneisha Means, Kevin Jones, Bennett McNulty, Patricia Posey, Shruti Patel, Denva Gallant, Pallavi Sriram, Earl Aguilar, and Lee Pierce. Lee cracked a whip on me to write and was very funny at the same time. She really pulled me out of the nonwriting ditch! She told me just to open my document daily and put one word on the page. Taneisha is my writing sister, and we traveled our books together from beginning to the very end.

I need to note that I am an anthropology seed from Yolanda Moses, Diego Vigil, Leo Chavez, Robert Garfias, Kyeyoung Park, Alessandro Duranti, Nancy Levine, Edna Bonacich, Karen Brodkin, Mariko Tamanoi, Sharon Bays, Sang-Hee Lee, Michael Kearney, Lynda Bell, Juliet McMullin, Christina Schwenkel, Sally Ness, Wendy Ashmore, and Eugene Anderson. Thomas Patterson, Eugene Anderson, Michael Kearney, and Wendy Ashmore's spirited (read: nuclear) anthropological theory debates were enlightening. My brain was in a ping-pong game of different theoretical schools during this time. Yolanda Moses, Thomas Patterson, Diego Vigil, and Michael Kearney talked to this Chinese restaurant kid for hours and hours about anthropology. Thank you. Thinking about Yolanda Moses and Eugene Anderson brings tears to my eyes for what they did for me. How does one thank their academic mom and dad? When I talk actually it is Yolanda and Eugene imperfectly reflecting back to students. Their kindness got me to finish my PhD. All of these distinguished professors are the reasons *I Pay It Forward*.

These theorist scholars have deeply affected my thinking: James Scott, Ariel Dorfman, Eric Wolf, Sucheng Chan, Ronald Takaki, Arjun Appadurai, Leslie Sklair, Michel Foucault, and *especially* Aihwa Ong.

I would like to thank all my Fresno colleagues, but especially Dvera Saxton, Thomas Ellis, Jill Fields, Veena Howard, Chi-Hao Wang, Tammy Lau, Hiromi Kubo, Matt Doyle, Henry Delcore, John Pryor, Chelsey Juarez, Yang Sao Xiong, Amrit Deol, Seng Vang, Amanda Cockerham, Isabella Lo, Diana Chandara, Lisa Wilson, Amber Crowell, Jennifer Miele, Vinh Nguyen, Samuel Contreras, and Shimel Her Saychou.

Thanks to my colleagues who fought against Asian hate with me: Timothy Fong, Simon Kim, Kim Geron, Russell Jeung, David Low, Leroy Morishita, Vang Vang, and the indomitable Virginia Loh-Hagan. I will scrap with you any day of the week for Asian American students.

At the very last minute and seconds of this book's completion a brilliant artist came in and gave me her wondrous illustrations. Her name is Sally Campbell Pirie (*formerly* Galman), and my soul is deeply grateful for her. She called this book a "jewel box" when I got worried it was too short. Alas, not sure if these words are true but they got me to the finish line. I want to thank all the artists in this book such as Allyssa Wu.

I would like to thank my wonderful research assistants over the years: Sanjay Soundarajan, Anou Vang, Katie Xiong, Hnub Lee, Madeline De Leon, Patricia Yang, Jessica Allred, Brandon Valiquilar, Sarah Vue, and *especially* Pedram Meymand. Pedram's one-percent multivariate intelligence is so appreciated, but his kindness is what I will forever remember. I also want to thank Nicole Hayward for his artistry.

I could not survive as a person without my girlfriends whom I met in eighth grade (Jennifer Chang, Lia Guntle), at UCLA (Kim Tran, Ly Phan, Judy Liu, Ruby Chen), at CGU (Herbert Ruffin II, Christina Owens), at UCR (Sandra Xochipiltecatl, Silvia Ventura Luna, Jelena Radovic, Holly Okonkwo, Vanessa Stout, Danessa Murdock), and at Chaffey (Allison Tripp).

I thank all my six generations of ancestors and descendants and especially my late mother (Nancy Banh née Ng) and father (Chuck Banh) who escaped war to survive and worked to the bone so I could have opportunities. My sister Christina Banh and her husband David Yu were critical to me in translations and generous spirit. My lab-boxer mix Bella and corgi demon Honey also got me through this pandemic.

There is no light on earth without Sean Slusser, Maxwell Slusser-Banh, and Alexandra Slusser-Banh. Oh, the global adventures we have had. #Grateful

Notes

Preface

1. I wrote about my family in Banh (2019).

Introduction

1. See Associated Press (2001).

Chapter 1   Indigenizing Consumption

1. Sea Shepherd is a U.K.-registered activist marine conservation charity that protests the killing of animals and marine life and works to protect habitats and oceans.

Chapter 2   Labor Indigenization

1. Pseudonyms are used for all employee names. These semiformal interviews were conducted outside the park.
2. See Arjun Appadurai's (1990) definition of indigenization.
3. It is not easy to be hired as a skilled foreign worker in Hong Kong; a prospective worker must fulfill certain requirements and obtain government approval. The worker has to have expert knowledge that cannot be provided by a Hong Kong local. Filipino dancers

and singers are common in Hong Kong because there is a lack of local talent in this field.
4. Another *Simpsons* episode was removed from Hong Kong streaming in 2021; it referred to the 1989 Tiananmen Square massacre.

Chapter 3 Spatial Indigenization

1. The story goes that in ancient China there was a man whose wife was having an affair with a tailor. The wife had the tailor make her husband a green hat to wear whenever he was traveling. The tailor would then know when the husband was gone and it was safe to engage in the affair. Soon the whole town knew, and thus Chinese men never wear green hats.
2. Karal Ann Marling (1997) explains how Disney's architecture is used to evoke a sanitized nostalgic past that is free from inequalities.
3. See "Garden of Wonders" at https://disney.fandom.com/wiki/Garden_of_Wonders.

Epilogue

1. Adapted from Milne 1928.

References

Abbas, Ackbar. 1997. *Hong Kong: Culture and the Politics of Disappearance*. Minneapolis: University of Minnesota Press. http://www.jstor.org/stable/10.5749/j.ctttshbm.

Abeza, Dawit. 2022. "Victorian Art History, Characteristics, & Style." *ATX Fine Arts*, April 23, 2022. https://www.atxfinearts.com/blogs/news/victorian-art.

Adams, Heather. 2023. "Hong Kong Disneyland: A Complete Guide." *WDW Magazine*, July 28, 2023. https://www.wdw-magazine.com/hong-kong-disneyland-a-complete-guide/.

Agence France-Presse in Hong Kong. 2013. "Hongkongers Still 'Negative' about Mainland Visitors, HKU Poll Shows." *South China Morning Post*, December 5, 2013. https://www.scmp.com/news/hong-kong/article/1372980/hongkongers-still-negative-about-mainland-visitors-hku-poll-shows.

Allison, Anne. 2006. *Millennial Monsters: Japanese Toys and the Global Imagination*. Berkeley: University of California Press.

American Chamber of Commerce in Hong Kong. 2022. "Michael Moriarty." https://www.amcham.org.hk/board/michael-moriarty.

Anderson, Eugene N. 1988. *The Food of China*. New Haven, CT: Yale University Press.

Appadurai, Arjun. 1990. "Disjuncture and Difference in the Global Cultural Economy." *Theory, Culture & Society* 7 (2–3): 295–310. https://doi.org/10.1177/026327690007002017.

———. 1996. *Modernity at Large: Cultural Dimensions of Globalization*. Minneapolis: University of Minnesota Press.

Associated Press. 2001. "Dredging at Disney Site Yields WWII-Era Bombs." *Deseret News*, February 5, 2001. https://www.deseret.com/2001/2/5/19567697/dredging-at-disney-site-yields-wwii-era-bombs.

———. 2005. "Disney Applies Feng Shui to Hong Kong Park." *AP News*, June 27, 2005. https://www.wfmynews2.com/article/news/disney-applies-feng-shui-to-hong-kong-park/83-403807425.

Banh, Jenny. 2019a. "'I Have an Accent in Every Language I Speak!' Shadow History of One Chinese Family's Multigenerational Transnational Migrations." *Genealogy* 3 (3): 36. https://doi.org/10.3390/genealogy3030036.

———. 2019b. "Workers' View on Indigenization of Theme Park: A Case Study in Hong Kong." *International Journal of Business Anthropology* 9 (1). https://doi.org/10.33423/ijba.v9i1.2225.

———. 2020a. "#MakeMulanRight: Retracing the Genealogy of Mulan from Ancient Chinese Tale to Disney Classic." In Roberts, *Recasting the Disney Princess*, 147–162.

———. 2020b. "Moana: Daughter of the Chief and Polynesian (in)Visibility." In Roberts, *Recasting the Disney Princess*, 129–146.

Barboza, David, and Brooks Barnes. 2016. "How China Won the Keys to Disney's Magic Kingdom." *New York Times*, June 14, 2016. https://www.nytimes.com/2016/06/15/business/international/china-disney.html.

Baudrillard, Jean. 1994. *Simulacra and Simulation*. Translated by Sheila Faria Glaser. Ann Arbor: University of Michigan Press.

Baxter, Tony. 1992. "Euro Disneyland, Fantasyland, and Frontierland." *Connaissance des Arts*, April, 62–71, 76–81.

BBC News. 2005. "Dogs' Fate Gnaws at HK Disneyland." July 26, 2005. http://news.bbc.co.uk/1/hi/business/4717347.stm.

———. 2018. "World War Two Bomb in Hong Kong Defused by Police." February 1, 2018. https://www.bbc.com/news/world-asia-china-42899251.

Bergstresser, Sara M. 2022. "Baby Milk and Boundary Transgressions at the Hong Kong–Mainland China Interface." *Anthropology News*, November 7, 2022. https://www.anthropology-news.org/articles/baby-milk-and-boundary-transgressions-at-the-hong-kong-mainland-china-interface/.

Bonacich, Edna, and Richard P. Appelbaum. 2000. *Behind the Label: Inequality in the Los Angeles Apparel Industry*. Berkeley: University of California Press.

Bosker, Bianca. 2013. *Original Copies: Architectural Mimicry in Contemporary China*. Honolulu: University of Hawaii Press.

Bourdieu, Pierre. 1984. *Distinction: A Social Critique of the Judgment of Taste*. London: Routledge.

Bradsher, Keith. 2004. "Disney Tailors Hong Kong Park for Cultural Differences." *New York Times*, October 13, 2004. https://www.nytimes.com/2004/10/13/business/worldbusiness/disney-tailors-hong-kong-park-for-cultural.html.

———. 2005. "Hong Kong Disneyland Is in the Soup." *New York Times*, June 16, 2005. https://www.nytimes.com/2005/06/16/business/worldbusiness/hong-kong-disneyland-is-in-the-soup.html.

———. 2006. "It's a Small Park: Hong Kong Disneyland Faces Overcrowding." *New York Times*, September 8, 2006. https://www.nytimes.com/2005/09/08/business/worldbusiness/its-a-small-park-hong-kong-disneyland-faces.html.

———. 2007. "Hong Kong Tries to Stop Mainlander Baby Boom." *New York Times*, January 21, 2007. https://www.nytimes.com/2007/01/21/world/asia/21hong.html.

Brandon, Elissaveta M. 2021. "Hong Kong Disneyland's New Castle Is an Architectural Vision of Diversity." *CNN*, March 26, 2021. https://www.cnn.com/style/article/disneyland-castle-of-magic-dreams-diversity/index.html.

Brigante, Ricky. 2013. "Story behind Mystic Manor: Imagineers Get Inspired by Classic Dark Rides to Create New Adventures for Hong Kong Disneyland." *Inside the Magic*, May 13, 2013.

https://insidethemagic.net/2013/05/story-behind-mystic-manor-imagineers-get-inspired-by-classic-dark-rides-to-create-new-adventures-for-hong-kong-disneyland/.

Brockenbrough, Marth, with Grace Lin. 2021. *I Am an American: The Wong Kim Ark Story*. New York: Little, Brown and Company.

Bryman, Alan. 2011. *The Disneyization of Society*. Thousand Oaks, CA: SAGE.

Burton, Sandra. 1999. "Exodus of the Business Class." *Time*, September 27, 1999. https://content.time.com/time/world/article/0,8599,2054251,00.html.

Carroll, John M. 2007. *A Concise History of Hong Kong*. Lanham, MD: Rowman & Littlefield.

CBS News. 2005. "Hong Kong Disneyland Opens." September 12, 2005. https://www.cbsnews.com/pictures/hong-kong-disneyland-opens/.

Cendrowski, Scott. 2016. "China's Richest Man Picks a Fight with Disneyland." *Fortune*, May 24, 2016. https://fortune.com/2016/05/24/chinas-richest-man-just-picked-a-fight-with-disneyland/.

Census and Statistics Department. 1988. The Government of Hong Kong Special Administrative Region. Hong Kong Annual Digest of Statistics. https://www.censtatd.gov.hk/en/EIndexbySubject.html?scode=460&pcode=B1010003

———. 1996. The Government of Hong Kong Special Administrative Region. Hong Kong Annual Digest of Statistics. https://www.censtatd.gov.hk/en/data/stat_report/product/B1010003/att/B10100031996AN96B0100.pdf.

Chan, Ming K., and Gerard A. Postiglione. 1996. *The Hong Kong Reader: Passage to Chinese Sovereignty*. New York: M.E. Sharpe.

Chan, Quinton, and Kang Chung Ng. 2011. "Ocean Park Trumps Disney." *South China Morning Post*, January 25, 2011.

Cheng, Albert. 2016. "Hong Kong Disneyland Has Only Itself to Blame for 2015 Losses." *South China Morning Post*, February 25,

2016. https://www.scmp.com/comment/insight-opinion/article/1916645/hong-kong-disneyland-has-only-itself-blame-2015-losses.

Chere, Lewis M. 1980. "The Hong Kong Riots of October 1884: Evidence for Chinese Nationalism?" *Journal of the Hong Kong Branch of the Royal Asiatic Society* 20:54–65. http://www.jstor.org/stable/23889546.

Cheung, Chi-Fai. 2013. "Big Leap in Bad Feelings towards Hong Kong Government and Mainlanders, Poll Finds." *South China Morning Post*, June 4, 2013. https://www.scmp.com/news/hong-kong/article/1253621/big-leap-bad-feelings-towards-hong-kong-government-mainlanders.

Cheung, Priscilla. 1999. "Officials Fend Off Criticism That Disneyland Deal Was Too Costly." *The Independent*, November 3, 1999. https://www.independent.co.uk/news/business/news/officials-fend-off-criticism-that-disneyland-deal-was-too-costly-740672.html.

Cheung, Sidney C. H. 2022. *Hong Kong Foodways*. Hong Kong: Hong Kong University Press.

Cheung, Tony. 2016. "Revamped Hong Kong Disneyland Set to Face Fierce Competition from Regional Rivals." *South China Morning Post*, November 23, 2016. https://www.scmp.com/news/hong-kong/education-community/article/2048578/hong-kong-disneylands-upgrade-and-cross-border.

Chiu, Stephen W. K., and Ching Kwan Lee. 1997. "After the Hong Kong Miracle: Women Workers under Industrial Restructuring." *Asian Survey* 37 (8): 752–770. https://doi.org/10.1525/as.1997.37.8.01p0272z.

———. 2004. "Withering Away of Hong Kong's Dream? Women Workers under Industrial Transformation." In Lee, *Gender and Change in Hong Kong*, 98–132.

Cho, Helen. 2018. "Bourdain, Off the Cuff: Hong Kong." *Explore Parts Unknown*, August 16, 2018. https://explorepartsunknown.com/hong-kong/bourdain-off-the-cuff-hong-kong/.

Choi, Kimburley. 2007. "Remade in Hong Kong: How Hong Kong People Use Hong Kong Disneyland." PhD diss., Lingnan University.

———. 2010a. "Constructing a Decolonized World City for Consumption: Discourses on Hong Kong Disneyland and Their Implications." *Social Semiotics* 20 (5): 573–92. https://doi.org/10.1080/10350330.2010.513192.

———. 2010b. *Remade in Hong Kong: How Hong Kong People Use Hong Kong Disneyland*. Saarbrücken, Germany: LAP.

———. 2012. "Disneyfication and Localisation: The Cultural Globalisation Process of Hong Kong Disneyland." *Urban Studies* 49 (2): 383–97. https://doi.org/10.1177/0042098011402234.

Choy, Philip. 2012. *The Architecture of San Francisco's Chinatown*. San Francisco: City Lights.

Choy, Timothy. 2011. *Ecologies of Comparison: An Ethnography of Endangerment in Hong Kong*. Durham, NC: Duke University Press.

Chu, Yin-wah. 2004. "Ming K. Chan and Alvin Y. So (Eds.), Crisis and Transformation in China's Hong Kong." *China Perspectives* 51 (January–February). https://doi.org/10.4000/chinaperspectives.798.

Coe, Andrew. 2009. *Chop Suey: A Cultural History of Chinese Food in the United States*. Oxford: Oxford University Press.

Cohen, Roger. 1993. "Company Reports; Euro Disney '93: $901 Million Loss." *New York Times*, November 11, 1993. https://www.nytimes.com/1993/11/11/business/company-reports-euro-disney-93-901-million-loss.html.

Collins, Eric. 2017. "Give It That Twist: The Allan Zeman Take on Life." *City Business Magazine*, April 2017. https://www.cb.cityu.edu.hk/CityBusinessMagazine/2017-Autumn/en/give-it-that-twist-the-allan-zeman-take-on-life.

Day, Kirsten. 2015. "Fengshui as a Narrative of Localization: Case Studies of Contemporary Architecture in Hong Kong and Shanghai." Doctoral thesis, Swinburne University of

Technology. https://www.academia.edu/14095792/Fengshui_as
_a_narrative_of_localisation_case_studies_of_contemporary
_architecture_in_Hong_Kong_and_Shanghai.

Defunctland. 2018. "Defunctland: The Failure of Euro Disneyland." YouTube, May 8, 2018. https://www.youtube.com/watch?v=SFE8R1K1LCE&ab_channel=Defunctland.

———. 2019. "Defunctland: The Failure of Hong Kong Disneyland." YouTube, March 22, 2019. https://www.youtube.com/watch?v=EdJi5jRLIgw&t=1s.

Dembina, Andrew. 2005. "Hong Kong Disneyland Opens at Last." *Asia Times*, September 13, 2005. https://discuss.micechat.com/forum/disney-theme-park-news-and-discussion/hong-kong-disneyland-resort/11317-greater-china-hong-kong-disneyland-opens-at-last.

Diana. 2023. "Top 10 Most Popular K-Pop Boy Groups." *Spinditty*, June 14, 2023. https://spinditty.com/genres/top-10-most-popular-k-pop-boy-groups.

Disney Concierge Services. 2022. "Tickets Store | Shanghai Disney Resort." https://www.shanghaidisneyresort.com/en/tickets/.

Dorfman, Ariel, and Armand Mattelart. 1975. *How to Read Donald Duck: Imperialist Ideology in the Disney Comic*. Translated by David Kunzle. New York: International General.

Dunlop, Beth. 1996. *Building a Dream: The Art of Disney Architecture*. New York: Abrams.

Eco, Umberto. 1987. *Travels in Hyperreality: Essays*. Translated by William Weaver. London: Picador.

Ehrenreich, Barbara, and Arlie Russell Hochschild, eds. 2004. *Global Woman: Nannies, Maids, and Sex Workers in the New Economy*. New York: Henry Holt.

Evans, Grant, and Maria Tam, eds. 1997. *Hong Kong: The Anthropology of a Chinese Metropolis*. Surrey: Curzon.

Fee, Margery. 1995. "Who Can Write as Other?" In *The Post-Colonial Studies Reader*, edited by Bill Ashcroft, Gareth Griffiths, and Helen Tiffin, 242–245. London: Routledge.

Forbes. 2007. "Allan Zeman: Hong Kong's Mouse Killer." February 13, 2007. https://www.forbes.com/2007/02/13/zeman-ocean-park-face-cx_vk_0213autofacescan01.html?sh=796f2eaa330e.

Foucault, Michel. 1977. *Discipline and Punish: The Birth of the Prison.* Translated by Alan Sheridan. New York: Pantheon.

Foucault, Michel. 1986. "Of Other Spaces." Translated by Jay Miskowiec. *Diacritics* 16 (1): 22–27. https://doi.org/10.2307/464648.

Fountain, Henry. 2005. "The Ultimate Body Language: How You Line Up for Mickey." *New York Times*, September 18, 2005. https://www.nytimes.com/2005/09/18/weekinreview/the-ultimate-body-language-how-you-line-up-for-mickey.html.

Frater, Patrick. 2005. "Mouse of a Different Culture: Hong Kong Theme Park Primed to Fly." *Variety*, September 5, 2005. https://variety.com/2005/biz/asia/mouse-of-a-different-culture-1117928496/.

———. 2016. "Wanda Hires Disney Executive Andrew Kam for Theme Park Division Variety." *Variety*, October 17, 2016. https://variety.com/2016/biz/asia/wanda-disney-andrew-kam-theme-parks-1201891709/.

———. 2020. "Hong Kong Disneyland's Latest Losses Blamed on Politics, Not Virus." *Variety*, March 16, 2020. https://variety.com/2020/biz/asia/hong-kong-disneyland-loss-politics-not-coronavirus-1203535355/.

Fung, Anthony, and Micky Lee. 2009. "Localizing a Global Amusement Park: Hong Kong Disneyland." *Continuum* 23 (2): 197–208. https://doi.org/10.1080/10304310802711973.

Gaudiosi, John. 2016. "Why Disney's New Shanghai Park Is Its Most Ambitious Yet." *Time*, June 16, 2016. https://time.com/4371493/shanghai-disneyland-park/.

Geertz, Clifford. 1973. *The Interpretation of Cultures: Selected Essays.* New York: Basic Books.

Gehrmann, Valeska. 2022. "Feng Shui." https://www.nationsonline.org/oneworld/Chinese_Customs/feng_shui.htm.

Gietel-Basten, Stuart Arthur. 2015. "Understanding Ultra-Low Fertility in Hong Kong." In *Low and Lower Fertility: Variations across Developed Countries*, edited by Ronald R. Rindfuss and Minja Kim Choe, 63–86. Cham: Springer. https://doi.org/10.1007/978-3-319-21482-5_4.

Gietel-Basten, Stuart, and Shuang Chen. 2023. "From Protests into Pandemic: Demographic Change in Hong Kong, 2019–2021." *Asian Population Studies* 19 (2): 184–203. https://doi.org/10.1080/17441730.2023.2193082.

Giroux, Henry A., and Grace Pollock. 2010. *The Mouse That Roared: Disney and the End of Innocence*. Updated ed. Lanham, MD: Rowman & Littlefield.

Glasby, Matt. 2023. "How Disney Got Kicked Out of China over Martin Scorsese's Kundun, a 1997 Movie That Ripped a Hole in US-China Relations." *South China Morning Post*, July 7, 2023. https://www.scmp.com/lifestyle/entertainment/article/3226599/how-disney-got-kicked-out-china-over-martin-scorseses-kundun-1997-movie-ripped-hole-us-china.

Groves, Derham. 2011. "Hong Kong Disneyland: Feng Shui Inside the Magic Kingdom." In Jackson and West, *Disneyland and Culture*, 138–149.

Hall, Stuart. 1990. "Cultural Identity and Diaspora." In *Identity: Community, Culture, Difference*, edited by Johnathan Rutherford, 222–237. London: Lawrence and Wishart.

Hills, Jonathan, and Richard Welford. 2006. "Dilemmas or Debacles? A Case Study of Disney in Hong Kong." *Corporate Social Responsibility and Environmental Management* 13 (1): 47–54. https://doi.org/10.1002/csr.107.

Holson, Laura. 2005a. "Disney Bows to Feng Shui." *New York Times*, April 25, 2005. https://www.nytimes.com/2005/04/25/business/worldbusiness/disney-bows-to-feng-shui.html.

———. 2005b. "The Feng Shui Kingdom." *New York Times*, April 25, 2005. https://www.nytimes.com/2005/04/25/business/worldbusiness/the-feng-shui-kingdom.html.

Hong Kong Disneyland. 2009. "Annual Business Review for the Fiscal Year 2009." https://hkcorporate.hongkongdisneyland.com/pdf/AnnualBusinessReview09.pdf.

———. 2010. "Annual Business Review for the Fiscal Year 2010." https://hkcorporate.hongkongdisneyland.com/pdf/AnnualBusinessReview10.pdf.

———. 2011. "Annual Business Review for the Fiscal Year 2011." https://hkcorporate.hongkongdisneyland.com/pdf/AnnualBusinessReview11.pdf.

———. 2012. "Annual Business Review for the Fiscal Year 2012." https://hkcorporate.hongkongdisneyland.com/pdf/AnnualBusinessReview12.pdf.

———. 2013. "Annual Business Review for the Fiscal Year 2013." https://hkcorporate.hongkongdisneyland.com/pdf/AnnualBusinessReview13.pdf.

———. 2014. "Annual Business Review for the Fiscal Year 2014." https://hkcorporate.hongkongdisneyland.com/pdf/AnnualBusinessReview14.pdf.

———. 2015. "Annual Business Review for the Fiscal Year 2015." https://hkcorporate.hongkongdisneyland.com/pdf/AnnualBusinessReview15.pdf.

———. 2016. "Annual Business Review for the Fiscal Year 2016." https://hkcorporate.hongkongdisneyland.com/pdf/AnnualBusinessReview16.pdf.

———. 2017. "Annual Business Review for the Fiscal Year 2017." https://hkcorporate.hongkongdisneyland.com/pdf/AnnualBusinessReview17.pdf.

———. 2018. "Annual Business Review for the Fiscal Year 2018." https://hkcorporate.hongkongdisneyland.com/pdf/AnnualBusinessReview18.pdf.

———. 2019. "Annual Business Review for the Fiscal Year 2019." https://hkcorporate.hongkongdisneyland.com/pdf/AnnualBusinessReview19.pdf.

———. 2020. "Annual Business Review for the Fiscal Year 2020." https://hkcorporate.hongkongdisneyland.com/pdf/Annual BusinessReview20.pdf.

———. 2021. "Annual Business Review for the Fiscal Year 2021." https://hkcorporate.hongkongdisneyland.com/pdf/Annual BusinessReview21.pdf.

———. 2022. "Annual Business Review for the Fiscal Year 2022." https://hkcorporate.hongkongdisneyland.com/pdf/AnnualBusinessReview22.pdf.

———. 2023. "Annual Business Review for the Fiscal Year 2023." https://hkcorporate.hongkongdisneyland.com/pdf/Annual BusinessReview23.pdf.

Hong Kong Government. 1999. "Briefing Paper Hong Kong Disneyland—Legco." https://www.legco.gov.hk/yr99-00/english/hc/papers/brief.pdf.

———. 2005a. "Chief Executive Speech during Opening of Hong Kong Disneyland." September 12, 2005. https://www.info.gov.hk/gia/general/200509/12/P200509120142.htm.

———. 2005b. "Speech by CE at Opening of Hong Kong Disneyland." September 12, 2005. https://www.info.gov.hk/gia/general/200509/12/P200509120142.htm.

Hui, Sylvia. 2005. "Disney Uses Feng Shui to Build Mickey's Kingdom in Hong Kong." *Las Vegas Sun*, September 8, 2005. https://lasvegassun.com/news/2005/sep/08/disney-uses-feng-shui-to-build-mickeys-kingdom-in-/.

IMDB. n.d. "TV Series, Animation, Anime, Japanese." Accessed September 26, 2023. https://www.imdb.com/search/title/?title_type=tv_series&genres=animation&keywords=Anime&languages=ja.

Jackson, Kathy Merlock, and Mark I. West, eds. 2011. *Disneyland and Culture: Essays on the Parks and Their Influence*. Jefferson, NC: McFarland.

Judd, Dennis R., and Susan S. Fainstein, eds. 1999. *The Tourist City*. New Haven, CT: Yale University Press.

Keatley, Robert. 1999. "We Have to Shift from Usual Sources of Wealth: Chief." *South China Morning Post*, November 3, 1999. https://www.scmp.com/article/298553/we-have-shift-usual-sources-wealth-chief.

Keegan, Matthew. 2020. "How Hong Kong Got Its Name." *Culture Trip*, January 28, 2020. https://theculturetrip.com/asia/china/hong-kong/articles/how-hong-kong-got-its-name.

Kim, Hye-Ryoung, Choi-Kyu Park, Youn-Jeong Lee, Gye-Hyeong Woo, Kyoung-Ki Lee, Jae-Ku Oem, Seong-Hee Kim, Young-Hwa Jean, Yu-Chan Bae, Soon-Seek Yoon, In-Soon Roh, Ok-Mi Jeong, Ha-Young Kim, Jeong-Soo Choi, Jae-Won Byun, Yun-Kyung Song, Jun-Hun Kwon, and Yi-Seok Joo. 2010. "An Outbreak of Highly Pathogenic H5N1 Avian Influenza in Korea, 2008." *Veterinary Microbiology* 141 (3–4): 362–366. https://doi.org/10.1016/j.vetmic.2009.09.011.

Kim, Jennifer, and Zhida Shang. 2023. "Research: How Anti-Asian Racism Has Manifested at Work in the Pandemic." *Harvard Business Review*, March 13, 2023. https://hbr.org/2023/03/research-how-anti-asian-racism-has-manifested-at-work-in-the-pandemic.

Kleiman, Joe. 2018. "Stephanie Young Named New Head of Hong Kong Disneyland Resort." *InPark Magazine*, December 7, 2018. https://www.inparkmagazine.com/stephanie-young-named-new-head-of-hong-kong-disneyland-resort/.

Ko, Vanessa. 2012. "Trouble Down South: Why Hong Kong and Mainland Chinese Aren't Getting Along." *Time*, January 24, 2012. https://world.time.com/2012/01/24/trouble-down-south-why-hong-kong-and-mainland-chinese-arent-getting-along/.

Koren, James Rufus. 2017. "From Bailouts to Boycotts, Saudi Prince Alwaleed Has Been a Longtime Friend of Disney." *Los Angeles Times*, November 7, 2017. https://www.latimes.com/business/la-fi-alwaleed-disney-20171106-story.html.

Kraar, Louis. 1995. "The Death of Hong Kong." *Fortune*, June 26, 1995. https://archive.fortune.com/magazines/fortune/fortune_archive/1995/06/26/203948/index.htm.

Lainsbury, Andrew. 2000. *Once Upon an American Dream: The Story of Euro Disneyland*. Lawrence: University Press of Kansas.

Lam, Sunny S. K. 2010. "'Global Corporate Cultural Capital' as a Drag on Glocalization: Disneyland's Promotion of the Halloween Festival." *Media, Culture & Society* 32 (4). https://doi.org/10.1177/0163443710369294.

Landler, Mark. 1999. "Mickey and Minnie Go to Hong Kong; a Proposed Disney Park Raises Queries on Tourism and Cost." *New York Times*, November 3, 1999. https://www.nytimes.com/1999/11/03/business/mickey-minnie-go-hong-kong-proposed-disney-park-raises-queries-tourism-cost.html.

Laris, Michael. 1999. "The Magic of Mickey." *Washington Post*, November 30, 1999. https://www.washingtonpost.com/archive/politics/1999/11/30/the-magic-of-mickey/35cbbc20-b77c-4a2b-9659-4448818dda7e/.

Law, Alex, dir. 2010. *Echoes of the Rainbow*. Mei Ah Entertainment.

Lee, Eliza W. Y., ed. 2003. *Gender and Change in Hong Kong: Globalization, Postcolonialism, and Chinese Patriarchy*. Honolulu: University of Hawaii Press.

Lee, Jennifer. 2008. *The Fortune Cookie Chronicles: Adventures in the World of Chinese Food*. New York: Twelve.

Legal Information Institute. n.d. *United States v. Wong Kim Ark*. Retrieved April 16, 2023, from https://www.law.cornell.edu/supremecourt/text/169/649.

Legislative Council. 2023. "Briefing Paper Hong Kong Disneyland." https://www.legco.gov.hk/yr99-00/english/hc/papers/brief.pdf.

Leung, Hon-Chu. 2001. "Overlapping Network and Flexible Manufacturing: A Structural Analysis of Hong Kong-Based Garment Industry." In So, Lin, and Poston, *Chinese Triangle of Mainland China, Taiwan, and Hong Kong*, 207–222.

Leung, Paggie. 2008. "Zeman Becomes Chinese Citizen." *South China Morning Post*, November 2, 2008. https://www.scmp.com/article/658776/zeman-becomes-chinese-citizen.

Leung, Ruby. 2017. "Time Auction Connects Young Volunteers with Hong Kong Leaders." *South China Morning Post*, July 25, 2017. https://www.scmp.com/yp/discover/news/hong-kong/article/3065488/time-auction-connects-young-volunteers-hong-kong-leaders.

Li, Amy. 2016. "Opinion: Why Are Chinese Tourists so Rude? A Few Insights." *South China Morning Post*, August 10, 2016. https://www.scmp.com/news/china/article/1251239/why-are-chinese-tourists-so-rude.

Li, Audrey Jiajia. 2019. "Hong Kong's Hatred of Mainlanders Feeds the Xenophobic Undercurrents of Its Protests." *South China Morning Post*, October 11, 2019. https://www.scmp.com/comment/opinion/article/3032041/hong-kongs-hatred-mainlanders-feeds-xenophobic-undercurrents-its.

Louie, Miriam Ching Yoon. 2001. *Sweatshop Warriors: Immigrant Women Workers Take on the Global Factory*. Boston: South End.

Lyne, Jack. 2004. "Hong Kong Disneyland Tops Out Centerpiece Structure." *Site Selection*, October 10, 2004. https://siteselection.com/ssinsider/snapshot/sf041014.htm.

Marling, Karal Ann. 1997. *Designing Disney's Theme Parks: The Architecture of Reassurance*. Paris: Flammarion.

Marx, Karl. 1992. *Capital: A Critique of Political Economy*. Vol. 1. Translated by Ben Fowkes. New York: Penguin.

Matusitz, Jonathan. 2011. "Disney's Successful Adaptation in Hong Kong: A Glocalization Perspective." *Asia Pacific Journal of Management* 28 (4): 667–681. https://doi.org/10.1007/s10490-009-9179-7.

McCarthy, William, and Ming Cheung. 2017. "The First and Last Signs of Main Street: Semiosis and Modality in California and Hong Kong Disneylands." *Social Semiotics* 28 (4): 443–471. https://doi.org/10.1080/10350330.2017.1304517.

McKirdy, Euan. 2018. "Unearthed Bombs Recall Hong Kong's WWII 'Black Christmas.'" *CNN*, February 2, 2018.

https://edition.cnn.com/2018/02/02/asia/hong-kong-world-war-2-history-intl/index.html.

Meacham, William. 2009. *The Archaeology of Hong Kong*. Hong Kong: Hong Kong University Press.

Mehrmann, Tom, and Michael Switow. 2018. *Taming the Mouse: How a Small Hong Kong Theme Park Came to Dominate Disney: 10 Lessons That Will Turn Your Business into a Success*. Singapore: Switow Media.

Mitchell, Bea. 2023. "Ocean Park Hong Kong Attributes $15.2m Surplus to Ongoing Transformation." *Blooloop*, December 13, 2023. https://blooloop.com/theme-park/news/ocean-park-hong-kong-surplus-resort-transformation/.

Mittermeier, Sabrina. 2021. *A Cultural History or the Disneyland Theme Parks: Middle Class Kingdoms*. Bristol: Intellect.

Moore, Ann. 2015. "How the Gold Coast Almost Became the Happiest Place on Earth." *Gold Coast Bulletin*, September 5, 2015. https://www.goldcoastbulletin.com.au/entertainment/how-the-gold-coast-almost-became-the-happiest-place-on-earth/news-story/fecafaf3c7bea8f69566a1f5c1b2997f.

Nackenoff, Carol, and Julie Novkov. 2021. *American by Birth: Wong Kim Ark and the Battle for Citizenship*. Lawrence: University Press of Kansas.

NBC Universal. 2023. "Tom Mehrmann | Leadership." https://www.nbcuniversal.com/leadership/tom-mehrmann.

Ng, Franklin, and David Nameth. 1995. "Feng Shui." In *The Asian American Encyclopedia*, 414–416. New York: Marshall Cavendish.

Ngai, Pun. 2005. *Made in China: Women Factory Workers in a Global Workplace*. Durham, NC: Duke University Press.

Nip, Amy. 2016. "Boss Won't Go Far from Park." *The Standard*, July 13, 2016. https://www.thestandard.com.hk/section-news/section/4/171529/Boss-won't-go-far-from-park.

Norris, Floyd. 2004. "Euro Disney Secures Plan to Ward Off Bankruptcy." *New York Times*, September 29, 2004. https://www

.nytimes.com/2004/09/29/business/euro-disney-secures-plan-to-ward-off-bankruptcy.html.

Ocean Park. 2009. "Amazing Asian Animals Now Open at Ocean Park." https://www.oceanpark.com.hk/en/press-release/amazing-asian-animals-now-open-ocean-park%20.

———. 2018. "The Two 'Made in Hong Kong' Brands Will Present Hong Kong's First McDull Music Theatre Show 'McDull Fishball On the Run' at Applause Pavilion, Ocean Park, Featuring McDull and Mrs. Mak." November 13, 2018. https://www.oceanpark.com.hk/en/press-release/mcdull-makes-unprecedent-appearance-at-ocean-park-christmas-sensation-for-first-mcdull#.

Ocean Park Corporation. 2001. "Ocean Park Corporation 2001–2002 Annual Report." http://media.oceanpark.com.hk/files/s3fs-public/ophk_ar01-02.pdf.

———. 2002. "Ocean Park Corporation 2002–2003 Annual Report." https://media.oceanpark.com.hk/files/s3fs-public/ophk_ar02-03.pdf.

———. 2003. "Ocean Park Corporation 2003–2004 Annual Report." https://media.oceanpark.com.hk/files/s3fs-public/ophk_ar03-04.pdf.

———. 2004. "Ocean Park Corporation 2004–2005 Annual Report." https://media.oceanpark.com.hk/files/s3fs-public/ophk_ar04-05.pdf.

———. 2005. "Ocean Park Corporation 2005–2006 Annual Report." https://media.oceanpark.com.hk/files/s3fs-public/ophk_ar05-06.pdf.

———. 2006. "Ocean Park Corporation 2006–2007 Annual Report." https://media.oceanpark.com.hk/files/s3fs-public/ophk_ar06-07.pdf.

———. 2007. "Ocean Park Corporation 2007–2008 Annual Report." https://media.oceanpark.com.hk/files/s3fs-public/ophk_ar07-08.pdf.

———. 2008. "Ocean Park Corporation 2008–2009 Annual Report." https://media.oceanpark.com.hk/files/s3fs-public/ophk_ar08-09.pdf.

———. 2009. "Ocean Park Corporation 2009–2010 Annual Report." https://media.oceanpark.com.hk/files/s3fs-public/ophk_ar09-10.pdf.

———. 2010. "Ocean Park Corporation 2010–2011 Annual Report." https://media.oceanpark.com.hk/files/s3fs-public/ophk_ar10-11.pdf.

———. 2011. "Ocean Park Corporation 2011–2012 Annual Report." https://media.oceanpark.com.hk/files/s3fs-public/ophk_ar11-12.pdf.

———. 2012. "Ocean Park Corporation 2012–2013 Annual Report." https://media.oceanpark.com.hk/files/s3fs-public/ophk_ar12-13.pdf.

———. 2013. "Ocean Park Corporation 2013–2014 Annual Report." https://media.oceanpark.com.hk/files/s3fs-public/ophk_ar13-14.pdf.

———. 2014. "Ocean Park Corporation 2014–2015 Annual Report." https://media.oceanpark.com.hk/files/s3fs-public/ophk_ar14-15.pdf.

———. 2015. "Ocean Park Corporation 2015–2016 Annual Report." https://media.oceanpark.com.hk/files/s3fs-public/ophk_ar15-16.pdf.

———. 2016. "Ocean Park Corporation 2016–2017 Annual Report." https://media.oceanpark.com.hk/files/s3fs-public/ophk_ar16-17.pdf.

———. 2017. "Ocean Park Corporation 2017–2018 Annual Report." https://media.oceanpark.com.hk/files/s3fs-public/ophk_ar17-18.pdf.

———. 2018. "Ocean Park Corporation 2018–2019 Annual Report." https://media.oceanpark.com.hk/files/s3fs-public/ophk_ar18-19.pdf.

———. 2019. "Ocean Park Corporation 2019–2020 Annual Report." https://media.oceanpark.com.hk/files/s3fs-public/ophk_ar19-20.pdf.

———. 2020. "Ocean Park Corporation 2020–2021 Annual Report." https://media.oceanpark.com.hk/files/s3fs-public/ophk_ar20-21.pdf.

———. 2021a. "Ocean Park Corporation 2021–2022 Annual Report." https://media.oceanpark.com.hk/files/s3fs-public/ophk_ar21-22.pdf.

———. 2021b. "Ocean Park Mission and Vision." September 21, 2021. https://waterworld.oceanpark.com.hk/en/corporate-information/.

———. 2023. "Ocean Park 2023." https://www.oceanpark.com.hk/en/corporate-information/vision-and-mission.

O'Connell, Caitlin. 2010. "Employee Suicides May Reveal Darker Side of Disneyland Paris." *New York Daily News*, May 6, 2010. https://www.nydailynews.com/news/money/employee-suicides-reveal-darker-side-disneyland-paris-article-1.444959.

Oh, Chuyun. 2022. *K-Pop Dance: Fandoming Yourself on Social Media*. London: Routledge.

Ong, Aihwa. 1999. *Flexible Citizenship: The Cultural Logics of Transnationality*. Durham, NC: Duke University Press.

Pang, Mary, Graeme Lang, and Catherine Chiu. 2001. "Impact of Plant Relocation to China on Manufacturing Workers in Hong Kong." In *Hong Kong Reintegrating with China*, edited by Lee Pui-tak, 109–128. Aberdeen: Hong Kong University Press.

Patrick, Anita. 2020. "Rwanda's Kagame Thanks Jack Ma for 'Huge Shot in the Arm' after Receiving Donation of Test Kits." *CNN*, March 22, 2020. https://edition.cnn.com/2020/03/16/africa/jack-ma-donate-masks-coronavirus-africa/index.html.

Raz, Aviad. 1999. *Riding the Black Ship: Japan and Tokyo Disneyland*. Cambridge, MA: Harvard University Press.

Ressner, Jeffrey. 1996. "Disney's China Policy." *Time*, December 9, 1996. https://content.time.com/time/magazine/article/0,9171,985663,00.html.

ReviewTyme. 2018. "The Troubled of Hong Kong Disneyland." YouTube, March 17, 2018. https://www.youtube.com/watch?v=F85-qqtxTo4&t=1s&ab_channel=ReviewTyme.

———. 2021a. "The Disney Park Walt Never Wanted—Tokyo Disneyland History." YouTube, March 21, 2021. https://www.youtube.com/watch?v=9i97JCqo_os&ab_channel=ReviewTyme.

———. 2021b. "The Unlikely Success of Shanghai Disneyland." YouTube, March 31, 2021. https://www.youtube.com/watch?v=nwEDN1Ynx8w&ab_channel=ReviewTyme.

Ritzer, George. 1993. *The McDonaldization of Society: An Investigation into the Changing Character of Contemporary Social Life*. Thousand Oaks, CA: SAGE.

Roberts, Shearon, ed. 2020. *Recasting the Disney Princess: The Coming of Age of the Empowered Children's Heroine in the Wake of Social Movements*. Lanham, MD: Lexington.

Rojek, Chris, and John Urry. 1997. *Touring Cultures: Transformations of Travel and Theory*. London: Routledge.

Ross, Andrew. 2000. *The Celebration Chronicles: Life, Liberty and the Pursuit of Property Values in Disney's New Town*. New York: Ballantine Books.

Russolillo, Steven, and Stella Yifan Xie. 2019. "Protests Have Turned Hong Kong Disneyland into a 'Ghost Town.'" *Wall Street Journal*, December 2, 2019. https://www.wsj.com/articles/protests-have-turned-hong-kong-disneyland-into-a-ghost-town-11575196203.

SACOM: Students and Scholars Against Corporate Misbehaviour. 2013. "Widespread Labour Abuses at Disney and Mattel Factories: ICTI Doesn't Care about Labour Rights Standards." http://sacom.hk/widespread-labour-abuses-at-disney-and-mattel-factories-icti-doesn%E2%80%9t-care-about-labour-rights-standards/

Said, Edward. 1978. *Orientalism*. New York: Pantheon.

Saiidi, Uptin. 2017. "Here's Why Hong Kong Housing Is so Expensive." *CNBC*, April 9, 2017. https://www.cnbc.com/2017/04/09/heres-why-hong-kong-housing-is-so-expensive.html.

Sassen, Saskia. 2001. *The Global City: New York, London, Tokyo.* Princeton, NJ: Princeton University Press.

Schlund-Vials, Cathy J., K. Scott Wong, and Linda Trinh Võ, eds. 2015. *Keywords for Asian American Studies.* New York: New York University Press.

Scibelli, Cathy. 2011. "Forget the Prozac, Give Me a Dose of Disney." In Jackson and West, *Disneyland and Culture,* 215–222.

Scott, James C. 1998. *Seeing Like a State: How Certain Schemes to Improve the Human Condition Have Failed.* New Haven, CT: Yale University Press.

Sims, Leslie, and Malik Peiris. 2013. "One Health: The Hong Kong Experience with Avian Influenza." *Current Topics in Microbiology and Immunology* 365:281–298. https://doi.org/10.1007/82_2012_254.

Sklair, Leslie. 2000. *The Transnational Capitalist Class.* Malden, MA: Blackwell.

So, Alvin Y., Nan Lin, and Dudley L. Poston, eds. 2001a. *The Chinese Triangle of Mainland China, Taiwan, and Hong Kong: Comparative Institutional Analyses.* Westport, CT: Greenwood.

———. 2001b. "Of Flesh and Blood: The Human Consequences of Economic Restructuring on Women Worker in Hong Kong." In So, Lin, and Poston, *Chinese Triangle of Mainland China, Taiwan, and Hong Kong,* 117–132.

Soll, Michael. 2014. "Mouse to House." *Global Gaming Business Magazine,* December 19, 2014. https://ggbmagazine.com/article/mouse-to-house/.

Sorkin, Michael. 1992. *Variations on a Theme Park: The New American City and the End of Public Space.* New York: Hill & Wang.

Sotheby's. 2022. "The Big Pigture: Life Lessons from the World of McDull." January 14, 2022. https://www.sothebys.com/en/articles/the-big-pigture-life-lessons-from-the-world-of-mcdull.

The Standard. 2022. "Hong Kong Disneyland Reports HK$ 2.4 Billion Net Loss amid Closure." March 21, 2022. https://www.thestandard.com.hk/breaking-news/section/4/188358/Hong

-Kong-Disneyland-reports-HK$-2.4-billion-net-loss-amid-closure.

Student and Scholars Against Corporate Behavior. 2013. "Widespread Labour Abuses at Disney and Mattel Factories: ICTI Doesn't Care about Labour Rights Standards." Scribd, January 7, 2013. https://www.scribd.com/document/119259449/Widespread-Labour-Abuses-at-Disney-and-Mattel-Factories-ICTI-doesn-t-care-about-labour-rights-standards.

Sun, Nikki. 2016. "Hong Kong Disneyland Drops Bombshell as It Announces Sudden Resignation of Managing Director for 'Personal Reasons.'" *South China Morning Post*, March 7, 2016. https://www.scmp.com/news/hong-kong/economy/article/1921963/hong-kong-disneyland-drops-bombshell-it-announces-sudden.

———. 2017. "'Unequal' Disney Deal Leaving Hongkongers to Foot the Bill." *South China Morning Post*, February 20, 2017. https://www.scmp.com/news/hong-kong/economy/article/2072406/unequal-disney-deal-leaving-hongkongers-foot-bill.

Sung, Ni-Chen. 2021. *The Glocalization of Shanghai Disneyland*. Abingdon: Routledge.

Sussman, Nan M. 2010. *Return Migration and Identity: A Global Phenomenon, a Hong Kong Case*. Hong Kong: Hong Kong University Press.

Themed Entertainment Association. 2018. "Theme Index and Museum Index: The Global Attractions Attendance Report." Edited by Judith Rubin. https://www.aecom.com/wp-content/uploads/2019/05/Theme-Index-2018-4.pdf.

———. 2019. "Theme Index and Museum Index: The Global Attractions Attendance Report." Edited by Judith Rubin. https://aecom.com/content/wp-content/uploads/2020/07/2019-Theme-Index-web.pdf.

———. 2020. "Theme Index and Museum Index: The Global Attractions Attendance Report." Edited by Judith Rubin.

https://aecom.com/wp-content/uploads/documents/reports/AECOM-Theme-Index-2020.pdf.

———. 2021. "Theme Index and Museum Index: The Global Attractions Attendance Report." Edited by Martin Pakicki. https://aecom.com/wp-content/uploads/documents/reports/AECOM-Theme-Index-2021.pdf.

———. 2022. "Theme Index and Museum Index: The Global Attractions Attendance Report." Edited by Martin Pakicki. https://aecom.com/wp-content/uploads/documents/reports/AECOM-Theme-Index-2022.pdf.

Tsang, Denise. 2018. "Boss of Hong Kong Disneyland Resort to Step Down." *South China Morning Post*, December 6, 2018. https://www.scmp.com/news/hong-kong/hong-kong-economy/article/2176709/boss-hong-kong-disneyland-resort-samuel-lau-step.

———. 2023a. "Hong Kong Disneyland Resort Records Lower Net Loss of HK$2.1 Billion." *South China Morning Post*, May 15, 2023. https://www.scmp.com/news/hong-kong/hong-kong-economy/article/3220574/hong-kong-disneyland-resort-records-net-loss-hk21-billion-12-cent-lower-year-year-management-voices.

———. 2023b. "New Pandas in Hong Kong? Ocean Park, City to Discuss Obtaining Pair from Beijing." *South China Morning Post*, May 10, 2023. https://www.scmp.com/news/hong-kong/hong-kong-economy/article/3219979/new-pandas-hong-kong-ocean-park-city-discussions-about-obtaining-pair-beijing.

Tsang, Donald. 2005. "Speech by CE at Opening of Hong Kong Disneyland." September 12, 2005. https://www.info.gov.hk/gia/general/200509/12/P200509120142.htm.

Tsang, Steve. 2020. *A Modern History of Hong Kong*. London: Bloomsbury.

Walt Disney Company. 2005. "2005 Annual Report." https://thewaltdisneycompany.com/app/uploads/ar-2005.pdf.

———. 2007. "2007 Annual Report." https://thewaltdisneycompany.com/app/uploads/WDC-AR-2007.pdf.

Watson, James L. 1997. *Golden Arches East: McDonald's in East Asia.* Stanford, CA: Stanford University Press.

Wiseman, Paul. 2005. "Miscues Mar Opening of Hong Kong Disney." *USA Today*, November 9, 2005. https://usatoday30.usatoday.com/money/companies/2005-11-09-hong-kong-disney-usat_x.htm.

Wu, David Y. H., and Sidney C. H. Cheung. 2002. *The Globalization of Chinese Food.* Honolulu: University Hawaii Press.

Yim, Bennett. 2010. "Case Study 1—Ocean Park: In the Face of Competition from Hong Kong Disneyland." *Strategic Management for Hospitality and Tourism* 2010:206–233. https://doi.org/10.1016/B978-0-7506-6522-3.00011-0.

Yiu, William. 2022. "Hong Kong Births Sink to Lowest in 56 Years, with Dire Implications for Workforce." *South China Morning Post*, February 28, 2022. https://www.scmp.com/news/hong-kong/education/article/3168599/hong-kong-births-sink-lowest-56-years-experts-predict-dire?module=hard_link&pgtype=article.

Index

accommodation, 3, 30
adaptation, 2, 46, 144
advertising, 52, 75
America, ix, xii
American cultural imperialism. *See* culture: cultural imperialism
amusement park, 101, 138
Anaheim, California, 10, 14, 35, 39, 44, 76, 85, 96, 97
anime, 52, 141
Appadurai, Arjun, 127
architecture, 34, 76, 85, 89, 90, 94, 105, 130, 136, 137, 144
audience, 47, 112
authenticity, 45
avian flu, 9, 71

Baudrillard, Jean, 77–78, 96
Beijing, 1, 32, 42, 152
bomb, 1, 76, 95, 96, 132, 144, 151
brand, 86, 101, 146

capitalism, 8, 13; racial capitalism, 106, 117
castle, 5, 15, 77, 95, 105, 133; Castle of Magical Dreams, 5–6, 94; Sleeping Beauty Castle, 95
cast members, 1, 15, 37, 64
Chan, Jackie, 88
childhood, 111
children, 10, 27, 37, 38, 49, 51, 52, 53, 81, 87, 97, 111, 112, 149
China, 4, 6, 8–13, 21, 26, 29, 31, 35, 37, 40–46, 48–50, 54, 60, 64, 66, 68, 88, 92, 98, 101, 104, 105, 116, 130–146. *See also* People's Republic of China (PRC)
Chinatown, 34
Coca-Cola, 68
colonialism, 27, 46, 52; colonialization, 42, 117; neocolonialism, 66; postcolonialism, 143
colony, 65; British colony, 8, 26, 40; Portuguese colony, 52
communication, xiii
communism, 13
competition, 13, 49, 77, 135, 153
COVID-19 pandemic, 67, 69, 111, 123
crowd control, 81
cuisine, 43, 44, 46
culture, v, xiv, 1, 3, 10, 23, 27, 28, 30, 40, 41, 45, 46, 49, 57, 74, 75, 87–88, 92, 138–139, 143; American culture, 108; Black culture, 123; cultural imperialism, 11, 71, 74; culture wars, v, 23, 25, 26, 28, 42; Disney Culture, 141; food culture, 46; Hong Kong's culture, 76, 81, 87–88, 98, 108, 131, 142; local

culture (cont.)
  culture, 74; popular culture, 51, 120; work culture, 60
customers, ix, xi, xii, 53–54, 70, 79

Disney, Walter Elias (Walt), 9, 11, 12, 108
Disney (company), 14, 27, 57, 74, 76, 77, 93, 152. *See also* Walt Disney Company
Disneyfication, 136
Disneyization, 134
Disneyland Paris, 12, 21, 35, 74, 76, 148. *See also* Euro Disney
Disney Stores, 4
Disney World. *See* Walt Disney Company
diversity, 120, 133
dreams, 108, 117, 133. *See also* castle: Castle of Magical Dreams
Duffy (Mickey's teddy bear), 2, 4, 32, 108, 113
Dune, xiv

education, 42, 103, 104
Eisner, Michael, 12, 93
employees, 28, 35, 58, 60, 62, 68–70, 108
environment, 9; environmentalists, 33, 36, 96
EPCOT (theme park), 10, 50
Euro Disney, 11, 12, 35, 74, 132, 136–137, 143, 145. *See also* Disneyland Paris

family, xi–xiii, 5, 26, 32, 39–40, 49, 50, 52, 73, 78, 88, 98, 99, 106, 114–117, 129, 132
fandom, 130, 148
fans, xiv, 4, 86
Fantasyland, 4–5, 117, 132
feng shui, 23, 34, 62, 74–86, 96–98, 132, 138–141, 145; feng shui colors, 82

feng shui numerology, 84
Foucault, Michel, 77, 127
Frontierland, 94, 132
Frozen, 86

gender, 58, 75, 135, 143
globalization, 132, 143, 153
glocalization, 143–144, 151
Great Britain, 8–9
Grizzly Gulch, 4–5
Guangdong, 32, 64
Guangzhou, 96

hallyu, 51
hamburger, 5, 112
handover of Hong Kong, 64
heterotopia, 73, 75–78, 98
hyperreality, 10, 127

identity, 46, 72, 139, 151; Hong Kong identity, 42
Imagineering, 11
imperialism: American, 27, 87, 93. *See also* culture: cultural imperialism
Indian, 5, 35
indigenization, x, xiv, 3, 23–24, 28, 31, 34, 39, 44, 72; indigenous competitor: Ocean Park, 99–114; labor indigenization, 23, 55–63; space indigenization, 24, 31, 73, 76, 98, 103
indigenous, v, 5, 57–58, 63, 71–72, 99
industrialization, 105; deindustrialization, 64, 98
investment, 15
It's a Small World, 108

Japan, xii, 4, 10, 12, 44, 79, 148
justice, xiii; injustice, 171

kawaii, 2, 10, 51
KFC, 43, 53

Korea, 45, 79, 142; Korean popular culture, xiii, 49, 51–52
Kundun (1997), 12, 139

labor, 3, 8–13, 20–24, 55, 57–72. *See also* indigenization: labor indigenization
Lantau Island, 149, 158
Lee, Bruce, 88, 119, 121
leisure, 88
lifestyle, 139
Lion King, The (1994), 12
Little Mermaid, The (1989), 12

Magic Kingdom, the, 10, 132, 139
Mainland China, 6, 8–9, 12, 21, 26, 29, 31, 35, 37, 40–41, 45, 48–49, 54, 60, 66, 68, 72, 89, 104, 133, 143, 150
Main Street, U.S.A., 1, 4–5, 11, 43, 57, 77, 88, 94
management, 14–15, 60–61, 139
map, vii, 2, 29, 75, 102
market, 35, 47, 66, 111, 113; marketer, 23, 38; marketing, 23, 33–40, 42, 46–50, 70, 74, 85, 107, 110–111
McDonalds, 26, 40, 43, 46, 53–54, 112, 153
merchandise, 14, 21, 32, 81
Mickey Mouse, 1, 4, 10, 32, 73, 81, 96
middle class, xii, 53, 145
modernity, 116, 132
Mulan, 4, 66, 119, 132
Mystic Manor, viii, 76, 90–91, 133
Mystic Point, 4–5, 90

nostalgia, 89, 101–102, 105, 114

old Hong Kong, 89, 105, 111
Opium War, 7; first Opium War, 8; second Opium War, 7
orientalism, 65–66, 87, 89, 95, 123, 149

Oriental Land Co. (OLC), x, 10
Orlando, Florida, 12, 35, 48

People's Republic of China (PRC), 3. *See also* China
Philippines, 60–61
politics, 131, 138, 143
Pooh, Winnie the, 25, 118
postcolonialism, 143
production, 30, 76, 85
protests, 31, 39, 42, 63, 88; labor protests, 29
public relations, 12, 21, 23, 38, 47; Disney public relations, 1
public space, 150

queue, 26, 27, 53, 70

racism, xiii, 142
reassurance, 144
restaurants, 5, 32, 34, 53, 112, 121

SARS, 9, 71
Shanghai, 12, 32, 45, 136
Shanghai Disneyland, 13, 20–21, 30–31, 50–51, 68, 149, 151
simulacra, 1, 78, 132; simulacrum, 57, 96
Singapore, 5, 45, 145
Students and Scholars Against Corporate Misbehaviour (SACOM), 65
synergy, 110

Taiwan, 29, 46, 105, 143, 150
tastes, 10, 22, 31, 43–45, 53, 102, 110, 133
teenagers, 26, 105
television, xiii, 35, 76, 78, 121
Thailand, 45
Tokyo Disneyland, xv, 2, 10, 12, 35, 148–149

Index 157

Tokyo DisneySea, 11–12
Tomorrowland, 4
tourism, 8, 34, 39, 48, 68, 76, 113, 143
Toy Story Land, 4–5
transportation, 13

Umbrella Movement, 7, 31, 39
unemployment, 9, 57, 64
union, 63–64
utopia, 76–78, 93–95

values, 93, 107–108, 149
Victoria (Hong Kong), 50
Victorian (style), viii, 2, 5, 73, 76, 85–88, 92, 98, 131
Vietnam, ix, xi, 5, 13, 79, 115

Walt Disney Company, 10, 14, 27, 57, 76–77, 93, 152
wishing well, 90
World War II, 76; WWII, 76, 95–96, 132, 144

About the Author

JENNY BANH is a keynote speaker, memoirist, curriculum developer, and award-winning associate professor at California State University, Fresno, in anthropology and Asian American studies. She received her anthropology BA from UCLA, her cultural studies (public policy focus) MA from Claremont Graduate University, and her anthropology MA and PhD from the University of California, Riverside. Her research focuses on Asian American studies, Asian studies, cultural anthropology, and Asian female characters in popular culture. She has published in *Genealogy* and *International Journal of Business Anthropology* and is the coeditor of *American Chinese Restaurants: Society, Culture, and Consumption* and *Anthropology of Los Angeles*. She also developed twenty-two new Asian American studies courses and the major at her university.